Come On Then

TERENCE OHAGAN

Bloomington, IN   Milton Keynes, UK

authorHOUSE®

AuthorHouse™
1663 Liberty Drive, Suite 200
Bloomington, IN 47403
www.authorhouse.com
Phone: 1-800-839-8640

AuthorHouse™ UK Ltd.
500 Avebury Boulevard
Central Milton Keynes, MK9 2BE
www.authorhouse.co.uk
Phone: 08001974150

First published by AuthorHouse 5/18/2007

ISBN: 978-1-4259-8031-3 (sc)

Printed in the United States of America
Bloomington, Indiana
This book is printed on acid-free paper.

"People see things different from other people and sometimes in a different light. I have written this book to the best of my knowledge and have no doubts, as I have stated in the latter chapter that I will have made a few mistakes.

There has never been any intention to cause any embarrassment or open up any old feelings from years gone by. If I have offended anyone then I do truly apologies for this inconvenience. This story is about my life that revolved around Huddersfield, if you read it and like it then the job as been well worth it, if you read it and don't like it, then all I can say is "you do one better", you can not please everyone is this world…………..

Again, I would just like to thank all the people who have given me help with this book and especially to those who have taken out the time to let me know just what a good book this has been"

Special Acknowledgements

To the Huddersfield Daily Examiner

For permission and use of photos and clippings.

Photographs

Daz Traverse, Chinks, Mumfie, Clanger, Big K, Irish and Carlton.

IT and computer work.

G.Parr.

A special thanks to Pat North and Zoot for the time on their computer while mine was down.

Interviews

The Silver Fox, Bullit, Syko, Ellis, Willy, Our Kev, AJM, Mr C, Daz Trav, Chinks, Carlton and everyone else to whom I am grateful with the other information that was supplied for the book.

Friends and acquaintances from over the years who have followed the Town and other escapades to which this book would not have been possible without them.........

The Golcar crew

Willy, Ellis, Max, Rick, Pabs, Mally F, Knighty, Our Kev, Milko (one punch), Blythy, Pido, Big K and his brothers Terry and Gaz, Capper, China, Ballbag, Clever Trev, Ziggy, Twiggy and Bob, Tim and Muggsy, Wayne (Slim) Sutty,

Dave H, Spock, Bruce, Ragtoe, Howey, Chris E, Pete, Mick T, Scotty, Carl, Pele, John Mart and Lowey, The younger end, Waddy, Wally, the two Barker twins, Ginger Nick, Poggy, Jimmy and Bar G, Syko (T) Welly, Wally, Mitch, Steve (chef) Zoot and Ears, Mally J and Brodie and the rest of the young lads of today

The Crew of old and the Townies

The Fox, Bullit, Syko, The four Nick brothers, Peanut, Paul, Martin and Dave Webbo, Goffer and Nige E, The Gouch, Nick, Doctor (F) Pete Nick, Big Phil Holmes, Westy, Irish, Icky, Chris Cass and their Kid, Paul Clav, John Mac, Knoppy, Sonny, Gassy, Butch, Yatesy, Gaz Dawson and his numerous brothers, Hammy, Bluey, Harry Webster, Batesy, Col Atkin, Ricky and Billy C, Dukes, Totty, Coffee, Kev, Booby, The original doctor (SO'M) Big Colin O'C, Pele, Harry Belefonte, Chris Pud, Chris Kelly, Welly, Barry, Mick and Pete G, Scoffer, Wilf, Jed, Ian L, Chimmy, Mick Basher, Joe, Milo, Oscar, Andy, Dave, Tatts, Patty, Middy, Dave, Eyes, Fountain, Donner, Poggy sue, Ali, Punny, Charlie, Dennis, Ash, Hightower, H and their kid, Big Batesy, Big Bruce, Scotty, The two Seans, Animal, Stavo, GPO 1 and 2, 3 star Phil, 2 broken legs Tony Calvert, PJ, John J, Joyce, Rob B, Dinxie, Mick Joyce, Shawie, Ronnie, Airen Cupboard, Mick Kenelly, Burky and the Irish fraternity, Mad Pete, Political Pete and countless, countless others

The Sheepbridge Crew

The Traverse Brothers, Clanger, Rob J and the rest of the boy's

<u>Brighouse and Rastrick crew,</u>

Mr C and his two brothers, Dallas, Nige, AJ, AJM, Mumfy, Locky, Junkie, Oscar, Daisy and the rest of the old boy's

<u>The Crosland Moor Crew</u>

Cally and his two brothers, Geordie Mick, Muggsy, Jimmy fingers, Lenny and their Roger big balls and the rest of this lot

<u>Heckmondwike Crew</u>

Dit Dat (come and get your brick back) Chilly, Simmy, Eddie one ball, Big Wilf, Tom, Phil McGowan and the rest of this barmy lot,

<u>Almondbury Crew</u>

H, their kid, big Steve, The twins, Tony Wilson and the rest of these boy's

<u>Walpole Crew</u>

Frank, Andy and the 3 Punching brothers and the rest of em'

<u>Cowersley crew</u>

Tom, Bert, Mackey, Phil H, Pete N, The Gouch and the rest of this mob,

The Crews from Brackenhall, Fartown

Lads from the Bradley and Birkby crews

Lads from, The Slathewaite and Marsden crews.

G. Hall (thanks for that night at Tranmere in '77) and the rest of the Cleckheaton lads

Gary B and the Dalton crew

The Paddock crew

The Oaks, Marsh and Lindley crews

The Kirkburton and Waterloo crews

The Newsome crew

The Ossett crew, whatever happened to these lads?

The Spen, Batley and Dewsbury crews

The HYC as it was then, with thanks to Chinks,

The HYS as it is now, with thanks to Carlton and good luck to J and the boy's, give it em' good style lads

All I can say it was a pleasure to have known you all and if I have missed anyone out, then tuff fucking luck

Thanks

Table of Contents

Foreword
Come on then!

Those three lovely little words, "come on then", the hairs on my neck used to stick up and the muscles tense, this was party time between two consenting factors and that was the cue for the off. We're Huddersfield and we're fucking proud of it.

I'm Tel boy, just one of the lads, no big hard man and I have been on my toes up the other end of the street a few times like countless others, who have been involved in this type of game. Our crew had no fancy name, we weren't all that big in numbers at times either, but we've fought them all, from the top to the bottom of England and they have known and have feared us. For the past Five years I have been wanting to write this book and now I have, to be honest, the last bit of inspiration I had was after reading Jaspers (Mark Chester) story on the naughty forty and also the sly grin from the Silver Fox, when I told him of my intentions, let's do it he says.

Like Jasper wrote, it's a case of where you start and what other people may say, but fuck it, I'm in the mood and we're on our way. This story like other stories on football hooliganism is about my life that revolved around the football from the late Seventies up to this present time, the good times, the bad times and the repercussions that it brought, the friends made and most of all the camaraderie that was involved. You may think that the stories that are mentioned are mostly about lower division clubs, but this is where it mainly then took place, but we have come across the big guns on more than a few occasions and held our own very comfortably and as you will see, we are also very much respected within the England set up.

I'm a chirpy happy go lucky chap who has always done quite well in life, the sort who falls into a pile of shit and comes out smelling of roses. I came from a working class background and was the man of the house in my young teens, my father was a great man but he loved the beer and song, he was convicted of armed robbery and we had to fend for ourselves in terms of money and survival. I was not bullied at school, but because of my size I was a target and it's a case of what you want, be a "joey" or fuck them. Fuck them is the option I took, and with that became a confident mouthy little fucker.

From the first time I met Mark Ellis down at Leeds road till this present time I will always have great memories and am proud of being part of what happened and what we got involved with, looking back I would not change anything. This book is dedicated to all the friends that I have made over the years and especially to my family.

I owe a lot to my wife Tracey, David, Matthew, Lauren and Kierney my children, who along with my long suffering Mother have put up with the problems that I have bestowed upon them over the years.

Again a special thanks to all involved, especially Ellis, Irish, Fozzer, Bullit, Syko, AJM, Daz Trav, Carlton and Chinks with all the help and belief that they gave me.

A special acknowledgement and dedication to a great man who we lost in India in very suspicious circumstances.

Mick "Basher" Bennett. He was a great friend through the years and in his time was Huddersfield's top boy, sadly missed but never to be forgotten. R.I.P.

Chapter One

In the Beginning

My early recollection of childhood was that of any normal family in the type of environment of that era. I was the eldest of three children, Kevin was a year younger and our Mandy was six years the younger.

I was born on the fifth of October nineteen sixty, a Libran, a typical weighing the odds up person. We grew up in an area called Milnsbridge and moved upwards onto the Botham Hall estate on the outskirts of Golcar.

I can still recall a party type atmosphere where we always seemed to have a house full with people singing and drinking. It was at this stage of my life where I started to realise what life was about and started noticing things of difference to other families, like my father not being around, or as my Mother would say, "your father is working away" what she kindly forgot to add to that little sentence was it was usually at Her Majesty's Pleasure!

My Grandfather, who I shall always hold in high esteem, was a real tough man, he used to mesmerise me with his heroics from the war. He was in the Navy and saw a lot of action. He came from a big Irish family and was well known around the Huddersfield area. He was a hard working chap who always made sure there was food on the table and the bills paid before he would look at a drink. From stories told in later years, he liked a drink and was renowned for sorting out people who stepped out of line, an honest and good man to which as the old saying goes " There's not many of those left nowadays"

I can honestly say, that when he passed away, that is the first recollection I have crying and wonder if those old stories of camaraderie and the likes were the moulding in my sub conscious for the years to come.

We again moved back to the Milnsbridge district just before I was to move to secondary school. I have always done quite well in school but in my early teens I had a morning paper round and also worked in the butcher's shop after school.

I understood life more and it was at this time that my father had received a lengthy sentence for armed robbery, maybe these distractions were the reason that I never progressed any further at this point in school although I knew I had the ability and aptitude to develop myself. I often wonder if this was the start of my life and that other elements and maybe destiny were already moulding and shaping it out.

Royds Hall Comprehensive School was I suppose just like any other secondary school, although we had a rather large influx of blacks and Asians. In my first year I recall the fire brigade having to be called to sort out the warring ethnic fighting, this was the whites and blacks against the Asians, great stuff this for a first year I thought.

Friends were soon made and gangs formed with allegiances at that time to either Manchester United or Leeds United.

These changed in the earlier years dependent on who was beating who up and who at the time had the most coverage on TV with the violence which we were beginning to see on TV more regularly. I was in my latter years of fourteen going on fifteen when I first met a lad called "Willy" at the youth club; he was the cousin of my best mate who was called Steve "Nipper" Wood. Now Willy was a bit different and just a little older at sixteen and came from Golcar, he had that swagger could not give a fuck attitude and we became friends straight away.

It was around this time that experimentation in girls and beer was developing and Willy seemed to be an old hand at this. He seemed to know every little trick in the book and had that miraculous spirit of survival through life which through the years I seem to have inherited myself

Through Willy, I made another friend who was called Mark Ellis. Ellis was a devoted Huddersfield fan and was well known down at Leeds road even at that early age for his courage and getting stuck in.

Willy had been at this time having a running feud with a well-known lad who could be a bit of a bully from the gang who we associated with. Every time they met, they would end up fighting and it was getting a bit out of hand. Willy could look after himself but he was getting a little pissed off fighting all the time. Every time he did ok against this lad or on the few occasions got the better of him, he would come back and you could guarantee it was when the odds were stacked against Willy, like when he was in bed one night. Ellis decided to see what this lad was like and if he could fight someone who liked a fight also. It was arranged for the next Saturday that he and Willy would call in the café in the town centre where we congregated, to pick me up for my first ever match. Through conversation it would be implied that this chap was nothing more than a bully and Ellis would sort him out. That way no one would know that it was an actual set up. I was more looking forward to my first ever game with all the hype and stories that were beginning to filter through from Ellis. Saturday came and Willy was on his own. Ellis had that week been sent on a short sharp shock for three months at Her Majesty's Pleasure, it was for a football related offence and it was a sickener.

It was a while after and I was in town one Saturday lunchtime when I bumped into a girl from school who was on her way down to the match. As we were talking a group of about a hundred or so lads came into view, they were shouting and singing, they'd just arrived from the train station and it was Preston North End. She turned round and said, there'll be lots of fighting with that lot today, why don't you come down and watch.

So off I go, the long walk down Leeds road was mesmerising, the mob in front psyching themselves and geeing each other up, obscenities were thrown at small bunches of Huddersfield lads, the police have it under control and a waiting Huddersfield mob laying in wait are moved on to the jeers of this lot. We get inside the ground and are inside the main terracing. I was dumbstruck, it felt so unreal, the noise and atmosphere, everything is loud and I can remember looking around like in slow motion taking it all in, then zap, back to reality, it kicks off. The Huddersfield lads pile into the Preston who have come through the open end and into the terrace and make short work of them. Preston flee like rats on a sinking ship, fucking great this I thought, excited and also very anxious at the same time, small pockets of fights then broke out all over the place as the police tried in vain to stop it.

I had noticed a familiar face and what became his famous jig like little dance before he piled in to them, it was Ellis.

Fucking easy meat that lot said Ellis, who had just been involved in at least three separate brawls against Preston on that first day. What the fuck you doing down here, you with Willy, no I said, I'm with these, pointing to the girl and a few friends from school, fuck them he says, come with me, they'll be some more fucking Lancashire cunts to twat, come on it's kicking off over there, Harry Belefonte is in there…

So off I went and watched this new mate doing his jig and dance and shouting "come on then" then piling in like a mini tornado, I was mesmerised, I will never forget that day, it's stuck in the archives of the brain forever.

From that first Saturday my new "mate" Mark Ellis along with Willy would guide me through my early years and the enrolment of the up and coming young Golcar bucks which later gelled into our team.

These two gave me my initiation into football life. Willy ended up like a brother with our kid and me, he lived at our house for a few years and we shared everything through these times in terms of grief and happiness, money and life.

Ellis was well known within the Huddersfield mob, he was small but had no fear of anyone, he had a brilliant kicking lunge that on many occasions I have seen boggled the mind of logic, he could swing his boot off the floor from a standstill and boot someone in the gob six foot and over in height with ease, he was like a fucking monkey. From that day at the match, I have remained good mates with Mark, we have had a fair old few laughs over the years and I had the pleasure of being best man at his wedding. Ellis is still the same person now as he was then, it's a case of what you see you get with him, it's no airs and grace with this bloke.

He still goes to the matches and still has the occasional punch up, although his lunging kick with age has slightly disappeared. As well as the football, the other great passion in my life has been "Northern Soul" which Ellis introduced me too, although very agile at the old boxing moves, his dancing prowess is something to be debated over. Carol his wife and a lovely lass is also the same and when we meet up we never stop laughing at the antics we used to get up to. I remember their first house, which I used to stay over on Friday and Saturday nights. Fridays would always be the same, out for a few beers; it would then be home for a few tins and polishing our spider doctor martins. I used to need two pairs or more of socks being the little chap I am. We would analyse our match and debate what the odds were on a brawl and also look at the fixture listing to see who would be at it up and down the country on Saturday. Come the morning it would be down the town on the piss and down to the match, we would then meet up later with Carol and back on the booze up town and also a nightclub. Every Sunday without fail and religiously it would be the same Sunday dinner of Fray Bentos steak and kidney pie, loads and loads of mash and cabbage, depending on who was the soberest, depended on how lumpy the gravy was. I can't thank them both enough for my early upbringing into what I call the real world and will always be indebted to them.

Huddersfield was in the old third division at that time and back in those days we had a good following with some very handy mobs. Almondbury, Fartown, Brackenhall along with the Moor were a few to mention, we also had a tidy mob from Heckmondwike with the infamous "Chilly bus crew". Barmy as hell this lot were with the likes of Chilly, Simmy and Dit-Dat (come and get your brick back) heading this mob.

The main Town firm on away days was run by a lad called Tony (GPO) Callahan, who organised the buses for the lads. Tony was a top lad and if the action was there, you can bet he was at the centre of it, he along with his brother, Paul who was also known as "hatchet man Callahan", this name was bestowed upon him after charging the Brentford crew at the back of the stands with a hatchet so the saying goes.

One brawl that sticks to mind with Tony was when we played down at Watford; we took around one hundred and twenty to one hundred and fifty lads. Ellis had been caught in an earlier brawl that saw him receiving two black eyes.

I must have only been around seventeen or eighteen at the time and remember that a group of Arsenal boys, around a half dozen or so, all handy looking lads, they had started giving the mouth to me and Mark and a voice from above the terracing shouted,

Oi you fucking lot, leave the young ones alone and try with us lot over here, it was one of the crew from the GPO. Bus.

These Arsenal boys then started taking off there coats, jackets and jumpers and proceeded to walk into the middle of the town lot, pushing and shoving anyone in there way, all of a sudden, GPO and the boys smoothed them, these Arsenal lads put up one hell of a show and it was real toe to toe and knuckle fight, the odds were stacked against them and it finally paid off with our numbers and the law saved them from any further beatings, but it was a sight to see and credit were its due to them.

It was an adventure getting to know these knew lads, Irish, Gassy, Knoppy and Chris Cass, Sonny, Booby, Harry Belefonte, Pele, Colin Atkin, Ricky and Billy Copperwait and Harry Webster were a few to mention in my first days.

Billy is another good lad who was lost to the big C, R.I.P Billy. From these groups in the early days, other young emerging lads of the same age as me which in time were to be some of the best friends I have ever had, were the start of the moulding to be the main firm and the best in our eyes that Huddersfield ever produced.

As I have said, these times in the late seventies and early eighties were aggressive and fighting in and around local towns and cities were the trend for the day. We were a good mob and would always stick together down the town and again on stag parties or anywhere the need was.

My first real brawl was Bradford at home, you could not have picked a better team or a derby for what Ellis called my tester.

We met up in the town centre and went to the Plumbers Arms, just under sixteen I was and when the barman asked what I wanted I just blurted out "the same as them" fucking Tetley bitter, it was awful, but after the first couple of pints I could have supped cats piss and not known. This was the first time I had been served in a bar down the town and I was half pissed. We met up with the boys in central town at the Swan, Gassy, Sonny, Irish, Knoppy and loads of the other boys that we used to run with were all out, everyone knocking back the ale and really up for it.

The next it was all out and the walk down to a pub at the top of Leeds road, the Broadwalk. We were walking from the pub to the top of Leeds road and it was then noticed that Bradford was here, they roughly had the same amount of number. They had just walked over the road from the Friendly and Trades to the sports centre, our big lads gave the cry of Huddersfield and led the charge. We all followed, Bradford spanned the road and bobbed about holding their ground, then as we got closer I thought shit, this is it, slowing down as we approached the front line of their mob, but as in so many instances that I have experienced, except for the few occasions, one side usually bottles it and legs it, sure enough Bradford did not have it that day, as soon as the first fist and boots were thrown, half their mob legged it, it's an unfortunate situation but the other half got fucked, well fucked, there was no running battles, just pure violence and blood. I had not seen anything like it; yes the usual school fight and what I had seen on television but to be actually involved in such madness and mayhem was surreal. The look of pure hatred on the aggressor's face and the pure lust of exuberance once their victim was rendered helpless and battered was mind blowing. In a word it was scary

It lasted all of thirty seconds, bodies and blood all over the place, listen these lads came for it, just as much as what Huddersfield wanted it and in years to come, we have experienced the same scenario and the boot has been on the other foot, but fuck it, that's what happens, it's all part of the game. The old bill turns up and saves this lot from further punishment but throughout the day several skirmishes followed near and in the ground. I will never forget the three of us walking down Leeds road, we had become detached from the main group and these two blokes in front were Bradford, before I knew what was happening Willy had twatted one right in the smacker and it was off again. What a brilliant result and eye opener that day was.

Once the match was over, it was the big finale, as in these days of the middle to late seventies it was big lad turnouts. We had beaten Bradford and they were well up for it and also to make amends for the kicking they had received earlier, there must have been three to four hundred each side on the main Leeds road, a lot of noise and then the running starts, they run us, we run them, the law turns up, but because of the large numbers, it's impossible for them to stop it and skirmishes break out up and down the front lines. I noticed then that each firm keeps closely together to ensure that they know who's backing who up, then you get the smaller groups and loners, running up and down the line, charging in at the given opportunity and dispersing just as quick, in the end who ever has the bollocks and bottle usually ends up running the other mob, that day it was Huddersfield's turn, order by then is usually restored and it's a good job well done and off for a pint.

I'm in dreamland, what a fucking result. Everyone in the pub is laughing and joking and triumph reigns over the winning battle with heroes being named and so on. I was hooked; you cannot describe the rush of adrenaline of being involved in this type of thing and only those that are involved know. I was now getting on first name terms with most of the lads that stayed and drank around town and was beginning to understand that feeling of camaraderie that my Grandfather had talked about.

The 70s

Chapter Two
Old Dears and False Teeth

My first job after school was into an apprenticeship as an Industrial Chemist, very handily placed just down the road from where I lived. Pennine Dying Co. The Managing Director of the company took an instant liking to me and always referred of me as that "Bloody Zulu", this was in reference to my hair which at this time in fashion of the era was like a bloody afro cut.

My hair grew outwards and was naturally curly. After leaving school early with no qualifications I had just popped into this place on the off chance of a job. Lady luck must have been there that day, that or either they were that desperate. I was offered an apprenticeship and informed that I would have to attend college. I jumped at the offer and settled in quite well with my smug attitude and little white coat. What made it even sweeter was a couple of month previous to this, I had bunked off school and Willy had pissed work off for that day. We needed some quick cash and decided to nick some lead from one of the mill roofs and cash it in. We chose Pennine and planned our raid from the outer buildings at the back of the works. All was going well and I had a decent bag full, Willy being the greedy git he was, wanted that little extra and in doing so put the bloody roof in. His legs disappeared into the hole and I managed to get him. Laughing and screaming I pulled him out and looking back into the hole were two black faces, later to be known as big Danny and Sunny. "Wot da fuck yoot" in a Jamaican accent came bellowing at us, we scarpered up the back fields past the vicarage with our booty and looked back to see a big posse of workers looking for us.

What a laugh and a good day's drinking binge we had on that one. The laugh on Sunny and Danny's face when I eventually told them that it was a mate and me when the roof went in that day.

I thought I was Jack the lad in the early days with both Ellis and Willy; they certainly brought the swagger out in me. I recall meeting several lads from school who were gobshites and who shall we say also got a bit back because I now had the confidence installed in me. I seemed to go through a spate of fights in which I always got the upper hand, although on one occasion up Golcar I did not do as well as I thought I could have done and got splattered in a bus shelter by the Wheel pub. This in itself is not a bad thing. It also brings caution into the confidence, a good combination if used wisely. The first time I can remember being on the receiving end with the football is also as clear as the first kicking you give someone. It's certainly not the same feeling as giving it and what I have found over the years was the jokes and piss take when you copped one. It takes the sting out of it and at least you can laugh.

It was on a trip up to Darlington. I can remember thinking what a shit hole this place was, it looked dark and dismal and reminded me of a place from the fifties or sixties that you saw on T.V. The mood on the Hanson coach had been good with the usual party four casks of ale and bottles of cider being passed about. What I liked most was the atmosphere on the coach on our away days. You had fifty lads who all knew each other and as soon as the beer wore in and the destination of your journey was on the horizon, the songs would kick in and the mood would become aggressive. What was happening here is the male ego trip and the ancestral caveman built in survival instincts as well as the defensive warrior cry, we are on enemy land and we are here to take you, listen to us, male bonding before they actually came up with it. We approach the town centre and the coach window goes through, the coach is stopped and we were off. Only around twelve to fifteen of us had managed to get off and we chased this mob into the town centre and realised that they had now run into a pub. We stormed the doorway and a good little battle erupted in the doorway. All I can see is Ellis' boot in the air.

One of the lads then came up and smashed the pub big front window with a breeze block of some description as a group of their lads were giving it with the fingers and gestures. As it went through it all then went quiet, then what seemed seconds, the entire pub emptied and they soon realised they outnumbered us overwhelmingly. They had expected a full coach load and found only a dozen or so. A fast and furious fistfight erupted with all the lads holding it, we were fanned out across the road and trying to hold it, but with the numbers being so overwhelming, we had no choice but to start legging it down the road.

I was unlucky, they copped me and although at first I did not seem to be getting hurt as they ragged me up and down with the amount of lads that had hold of me, the next thing I knew I was waking up at the side of the road with two old dears smacking these lads with their handbags! They then got me into another pub; got me a beer and a woman police office came in and questioned me over the window

What I did not know was that when I went down Ellis and Irish realised further down the road that I was not with them and they came firing back into this group who had kept on chasing them. The other lads followed but the law was hell bent on having one of them for the window. They could not see me anywhere (I was having a beer with the two old dears that saved me) and had to leg it again. It was a long walk to the ground and a couple of times I had to look at the floor and count my blessings. The mob that had turned us over were still hanging about and wanted another piece of my arse, two Geordie lasses walked with me after I had asked the way to the ground. We turned around the corner and a mouthy blond haired lad was heading this mob. As we became level with them, they approached me and the two girls turned on them without any hesitation and gave them hell. All the time I was getting the offer and an odd smack on the head, but credit to the two girls who several times flew into this mob and saved my arse. The sanctuary of the ground was soon there and the Huddersfield lads were all over the place as usual. We have always had a good away following and still have to this present day.

Ellis and Irish had a good laugh when I explained what had happened and they were giving me a bit of stick over it. Their ground was shit, a small tin shed for the away fans and a wooden sort of stand around the corner. They seemed to have a decent sort of mob and the ground was easy accessible all round with not much law about. It was one of those places that you know that trouble would happen somewhere along the way. I can't recall why but we took someone to the Saint John ambulance shed for some reason or other and just around the side at the back of this stand to the right, was the mouthy blond fucker with several of his mates. That's the twat I said to Ellis, right he says, let's fucking have 'em, it was equal numbers and before they knew it, blondie was on his arse and most of his mates did one and I had great pleasure in letting him know what the crack was on even numbers, as my boot crashed against his head several times. Whoever coined that phrase "revenge is sweet" would have got a pint from me that day. Funny situations these, seen it a few times, Mr Big Mouthy giving it large when he's mob handed, funny how they soon change their tune and start wailing when they get a bit back, these are the same sort who go crying to the law. Should not be in this game if that's the case, you give a beating and get a result or you take a beating and think, next time. Another thing that springs to mind also about that place was that when we went back to the coach after the match, a small reception committee was waiting, I don't know why they bothered, as soon as we go to them they scatter, one lad even ran and jumped into a river in a built up seventies style block walling of some sorts to get away from the lads. Why do these mobs do this, at least show some face and have a go if that is what you want. I really enjoyed this part of my youth with the new friends I had and really looked forward to these weekends.

I was now coming of age and it was soon my eighteenth and we had a bit of a do at the Prospect in Longwood, I had my leg in plaster from playing football at my new place of work. As the apprenticeship was not paying much, I decided to fuck them off; well it may have been more like they'd found out about my court appearance first. I had managed to get into a place called Longwood Finishing that our Kevin and Willy worked at. It paid nearly three times as much and was a lot easier. We always played football through the dinnertime and a lad called Ricky, who I have spent many a good year with, decided to give me a few days off work before my eighteenth birthday with a knacked leg whilst play footie at dinner time the day before. He smashed all my tendons and I was strapped up and on crutches for three weeks.

The party passed pleasantly and all the lads did me proud by turning out. This as my life history will unfold must have been the only party where no one was arrested or nearly killed. Parties and me do not mix and the gods above must have taken pity on my eighteenth with me already on crutches and knacked leg. Life was going easy and with Ellis being married. Willy and I seemed to spend more time without him although he was still there at the match days.

The FA Cup and other cups are brilliant, it gives you chance to pull one of the big ones and we drew Bolton Wanderers down at Leeds road in the FA Cup fourth round. For some reason I cannot recall why I did not go down to the match with Ellis. I arrived in the town centre looking at what was going on, I walked with a couple of the lads into St George's square and saw around forty of the main Huddersfield lads having it out with a vastly superior in numbers wanderers firm, they were giving the lads a bit and the law turns up to save the day, people split into small groups and are disappearing up alley-ways and into pubs.

Bolton are all over the place and are well up for it, I make my way down to the ground on the bus, seeing the odd punch up on the way down Leeds road. As I have stated earlier, it's mostly the lower divisions and I am not used to see the amount that these lot have brought over, we are outnumbered all over on the way down. Outside the ground by the Shed, a massive group of Bolton are hanging around, one shouts over to me, I'm having those docs off you after the match you little twat, fuck this I thought and got into the ground sharpish. In the ground it seems as though this fucking lot have brought an army over, there are thousands of the fuckers. We are in the "shed" and stood next to the railings next to the main terracing triangle area. Both sets of fans are goading each other and hot oxo is flying between the two groups, all of a sudden, a massive gap appears at the bottom end. Bodies start flying everywhere, I see the tell tale signs, the silly dance routine gives it away, it's Ellis and another lad from Golcar called Mick Kimmings. Mick has flown into about twenty of them from the back, he's a big stocky lad with good weight behind him and sends them flying all over, Bolton panic, fearing a mass of Huddersfield, but they soon realise that there are only two of them, by this time Ellis has fired in as well and they are doing very well to hold up against the numbers, they have the upper hand with the height advantage on the terracing steps and are windmilling like hell, eventually they are swarmed, everyone is trying to get over the railings to help, but the law is there and the two of them are arrested. What a walk of honour they received being marched past the shed that day.

It takes a lot of guts for two lads to fire into a massive number like that and the mouthy Bolton ones who were giving it at the railings before sure kept quiet afterwards, but that shows the spirit of Huddersfield and what we are made of.

You can't take it away from Ellis and as I have said, he still likes a punch up and loves it. Ellis still loves going to the away games and often ventures away with his lad, Jodie and his mates and informs me that they have had quite a few run ins and he still craves for it. He was at it with some local bouncers the other week in town, his lad ended up being locked up. Once it's in you, it's very hard to walk away from it, most people my age would not get involved and probably walk away, but fuck it he tells me.

I asked Ellis on his thoughts about it all and it's the same answer as the other lads, wouldn't change anything, we have had a lot of laughs, gave and taken kickings but that's what you expect. We have a code amongst ourselves.

I asked him which fight would he consider to be the best and sticks out in his mind. After a short while, he tells me it was Aldershot. "It must have been the year that they went out of the League I think. We had a decent mob and got to their boozer, they were really mad for it. It was the first time I remember knives being drawn, all tooled up they were. The pub was wrecked and the fighting lasted all day, I think they wanted to leave on a high. It wasn't big numbers or a big name team but they sure put on a good show and it was a case of you fought or got it bad, it sticks in my mind that one". He then states "I have had my fair share of arrests and the one that must have been the funniest was when we went down to Torquay. We had gone on the coach and arrived early doors. We had a good dinnertime on the beer and Willy, Knoppy and me were rather blotto and fell asleep during the match. Just before the finish, over the tannoy was an announcement that the coaches would pick the lads up outside the ground and not in the centre where we had been dropped off earlier. As we were asleep we did not hear this and after the match, we walked into the centre and found to our bewilderment that there weren't any coaches. Fucking stuck at the other end of the country with next to no money. Irish was in a mini bus and had two spare seats, but we agreed that as there was four of us, we decided to stick together. After walking around we decided that the only option was to nick a car, which we did. We got as far as Paignton where we were collared by the law. We got banged up and thrown out mid morning, we had to walk to Exeter where I called me ma and she buzzed us money down for the National Express. Going back to court was even worse; we had to go on the Sunday for the Monday court session. The coach did not return back till the Tuesday. We decided to sleep rough on some benches that we knew of on the pier and were woken by this chap. He turned around and said I could of killed you lads there if I had a knife and a conversation was then struck up. This chap offered us food and accommodation, which we took as it was better than nothing else.

When we got to this geezer's house, we were apprehensive anyway, but after the food he turns around and informs us that he only has two beds and that one of the three of us had to share the bed with him. After a lot of finger pointing and arguing between us it was agreed that"…. Unfortunately due to publicational rights and the two different versions to the ending of this story, I am not at liberty to reveal the indentity of the person who ended up sharing the bed with him but our Willy will put you right on this, ooops.

Willy had to have false teeth at a young age and a favourite pastime of his was to drop his teeth into someone who had just bought a drink, they would shriek and he'd end up having their drink more often than not.

It worked loads of times till one afternoon in the Wellington in town when he dropped them into this geezer's drink he just bought, the fella went for a drink and yelled, he picked the teeth out of his pint and threw them into the middle of the packed pub. The pub was in very dim lighting because a disco was on, the laughs we had while he was on his hands and knees looking for them in this crowed pub. This was also a trademark chat up line with the women; he would drop his teeth into their drinks just to break the ice if you will pardon the pun.

It was a pain sometimes, he was a handy fucker and could dish it out, but if a fight started he had a habit of giving me his teeth and saying, look after these. Fuck this for a game of soldiers I thought, what if the fuckers break and he blames me. This I recall was the first sort of falling out or argument that Willy and I had and we certainly have had a few more with swapped punches over the years. We have had more laughs and life threatening experiences than I care to remember, in and around the start of the eighties.

One of these experiences that we often laugh about was when we went into a pub called the Dusty Miller up Longwood. The fashion was turning back into skinhead type with the arrival and up and coming new bands about to appear with the Ska sound. We loved this and looked the part. The Dusty was a well-known bikers' pub but it was situated next to the bus terminus for our bus to the town.

It was full that night with some kind of party going on. Their top boy was a bloke called John "Father" Hammond, he was a great lad and knew us, we got a drink and went into the pool room, the table was full of money and we had about half an hour before the bus into town, the bus stop was just over the road. The bikers laughed when we asked if we could push in for a game before we went, they joked and said ok, a game of doubles. If we win, we get your arse holes, you win and we let you shag one of the girls as we all watch, then you walk away free, ok we said. This pub had a few small rooms and these bikers were all over the place, the game was half way through and about ten of them were trying to put us off with looks and the old, you've got a nice little arse skin boy, suddenly a fight broke out in the other room, they all left, I looked at Willy and said, let's do one, he laughed and said, fuck it, he took about a pound of the pool money that was laid down on the table, this will have them wondering he said, fuck it I said and took the fucking lot, this will get them going even more, around three and a half quid, we ran outside and jumped on the bus and ran upstairs. Willy said "get down, they are all running around looking for us outside", we hid underneath the chairs laughing, the bus did not move, it's at times like these when a minute seems an hour, we could hear the bus doors open, have you seen two little fucking thieving bald head lads the pissed off biker asks the driver, the driver who we knew "lucky for us" replied no mate, at that point one of the bikers ran up the steps, we were shitting ourselves something rotten, there was just a woman of around thirty on and just in front of us, "you on your own love", yes she replied, thank fuck for that our Wily said, the biker went, the woman looked and she smiled at our Willy and said, fucking dirty bastards that lot, always making a noise and causing trouble, stay down, they're still running all over the place screaming for your blood, that's the sort of thing we used to get up to, anything for a laugh us two and fuck the consequences.

Terence OHagan

The 70s

Chapter Three
Mad Dogs and Englishmen.

This term as we all know is about what most other countries think of us barmy Englishmen. Whilst writing this book I have come across some of the lads I have not seen for fifteen to twenty years. It's amazing what the old grey matter stores in your head and reminiscing with these lads from the old days brings it all back and when reflecting on these past experiences and what a barmy and mad lot we were.

Where else in this world at that time did you have hundreds of lads travelling up and down the country every Saturday in the hope of beating someone's head in or the wanting to kill someone? Most of all it's the laughs and situations we end up in are what makes these stories and I have countless that I could write.

Certain individuals keep cropping up again and again and it dawns on you just how daft and mad these lads were. On one of the many trips down to Torquay one story that keeps doing the rounds was when we arrived down there and the match had been called off. After a few beers it was decided to go to the cinema and watch the new movie out which at this time was Rollerball. While everyone was watching the film, Big Bruce then appeared from nowhere with an attendant's carry tray selling ice creams and chocolate, where he had got this from I do not know and the howls of laughter around the room were deafening. He did not sell much and I wonder if this had anything to do with the fact that he had his dick hanging out of his pants whilst doing this.

All the boys then went on the piss and ended up at a boozer called the Harbour. This was full of Hells Angels. This was one of those situations where anything could have happened and it did. One of the lads shouted, right you lot come on, outside. They did and a massive fight then took place, with snowballs. The game had been called off with snow and the sight of a group of Hells Angles and football lads snowballing each other must have been a relief to the watching people and police of this town.

There are also countless people I have not named from these days but they all played a part but a big mention to one of the top boys from this era and who I remember well and was a big name associated with the Town lads and was a legend in his own lifetime. Because of outside interests we are going to call him, H.

H now living in the Midlands still pops up and calls into the game, he his well known for his voice and the give us an H song which no one has ever managed to replicate. He put a lot into the lads and the club from an early age and he is well known throughout the Huddersfield lad's folk-law to this day. He always had his trousers around his ankles when he was pissed and had a knack of getting the lads going.

He has always professed to not being a hard man, but loved the camaraderie of the lads and his strongest point from what I saw was his motivation of the boys, which in some situations if you can associate with me at times is a great weapon itself. H used to be part of the old suicide squad as they used to call themselves and on one occasion down at Exeter when Town were losing three nil at half time they pissed off outside and had a game of football themselves while the match was still going on. Town lost by more goals and after the match around a hundred or so Exeter boys came looking for them giving it the large. Well pissed off at this the lads headed by both H and Irish charged up at them in the bus station, throwing petrol cans and any other weapon they could get their hands on. When all the weapons had finished the lads streamed at them, Exeter did not want anything to do with them and they legged it.

What I liked about this lot was that they would always look after the younger lads such as myself and this came true on many occasions, one in particular was down at Southend. We had arrived early and around thirty of us went to the nearest pub. We had a half mixture of young and old and it was not long before the pub was full of the Southend lot. You could tell that we were getting weighed up and we were well outnumbered. The older lot were keeping their eyes on us and a few of their boys had struck up conversation with us. The older lads kept telling us to watch ourselves and stay close. Nothing happened in the pub and half of the Southend had gone.

I remember thinking, this other lot are going to follow us out and the other lot will be waiting, as soon as we got outside Col Atkin, one the older lads started barking at us, right, you young ones all get to the front now, if it comes we all turn and us older lot are at the front. I remember thinking at least we have lads who look and care after the younger ones, it was no big bravado, but a genuine feeling that we also have passed down over the years. Nothing kicked off and we got to the ground in one piece. This place sticks out in my mind even now; it seemed to be a very steep open end that they had with loads and loads of steps in this terracing. In these days we all used to wear the six-inch platform shoes and trouser flares and all the other silly clothes of that fashion era. Most of us were congregated at the bottom part of this end. We were all laughing and joking when they came at us from the top. They sure had their tactics planned out and came streaming down at a fast pace at us. Panic threw caution to the wind and we ran, some of the older lads were trying to fight them off but with being so outnumbered and the advantage of coming down at us from the terracing we had no chance and the rest were also off. I can remember thinking afterwards what it must be like for a woman with their stiletto shoes as it was murder trying to run down those steps in the platform shoes and even worse trying to get onto the pitch. No one got really hurt and we really laugh on that one. The songs from the early days are always a good reminder of what happened and we were more proud of coming from Yorkshire than anyone one else. God's own county this place and proud of it

My first outing out of the country as I call it, was to Newport, Wales. This must have been the first time I can recall thinking how proud I was to be an Englishman. I have always been proud to come from Yorkshire but even though it was only Wales it brought out another venom of hatred that I had not seen before. The stories came true of how the Welsh have a massive disliking of the English people themselves when we went drinking around Newport. You could tell from their attitude towards us, it was not because we were football fans but because we were Englishmen and with the audacity of being in their country. Walking into the ground me, Ellis, Booby and Coffee ran into a group of these lot, I dived into them followed by the lads, it did not last long and the Welsh wankers were off. We had no other opposition from Newport that day other than seeing them at the ground waving their little Welsh flags. We were on our way back and had stopped at the service station when someone shouted, look at that lot over there. An army of lads with Welsh flags were storming down the banking at the other end of the motorway reservation. It was Cardiff. Even in these days these boys had a bit of a reputation and we were only too glad to see what they were actually made of.

The Town lads followed suit this end and stormed to the barriers of the hard shoulder. Ranting verbal abuse was being thrown from both sides, which could just be heard over the flowing traffic. Then came bricks and whatever else they could throw at us, the same followed suit from our side and by this time some of the lads were actually on the motorway gesturing for these lovely Welsh people to come and have it. All of a sudden a trolley load of knives and forks and all sorts of other things had appeared, possibly with the help of RJ landed at our side and these were soon to be seen flying over in the direction of these sheep shaggers who were now onto the motorway as we were. The traffic had by now been brought to a stop and battle commenced across the central reservation. This did not last too long because of the law enforcement bestowed upon both warring factions. We dispersed and went back to our coaches proud to be English. This episode along with Harry Belefonte's one-man attack upon the hated scum of the Leeds gelder end will be the ever-lasting memories from that era.

The 70s

Chapter Four
The Golcar

We had seen other lads from our area descending to Leeds road and it was not long before we were arranging to all meet up and organise as Max would say the G-Troop.

At one of the matches, Mark, Willy and myself bumped into a few of the Golcar Lads, Knighty, Ricky and a couple of others were the ones that I remember mostly. After the match we would sometimes go back up to Golcar and other lads such as Max, Pabs, Caper, Big K and Pido would be there.

Stories would be usually flying about and other lads would laugh and join in on how it would be great if we all went together.

It was then arranged that we would all go to Barnsley, a big derby match and to go on previous visits it was a sure fire odds on bet that trouble would be guaranteed. These Barnsley lads are no mugs at home or away and can hold their own.

The day dawns and it's Barnsley away and the new crew are loving it, stories of how in the past we have charged down the gates at the away end and got in for nothing and the reception we always get are flying around. We all meet in the Prospect pub in Longwood, a good turn out for the newly formed crew from Golcar, a good twenty or so of us, I won't forget the site of this mob walking out full of ale and ready for it, the younger ones as I call them were in fact only a couple of years younger, but were well up for it. We have some big lads with us and Ellis, Willy and myself are as proud as fuck.

A massive turn out that day from Huddersfield saw no reception committee from Barnsley, but the lads weren't to be out done, as people were queuing at the turnstiles, the lads decided that the gates looked a better proposition and Max led the charge on the doors, it did not take long before half of Huddersfield to join in and within seconds under the might and pressure the doors gave way, in we went laughing and jeering, we couldn't believe that the team started it all off and all the other firms were talking about it, which over the years, they would be talking a lot more. The lads loved it and once the whistle blew at full time we were all off. Barnsley whether it was guilt and to make amends for not turning up or had decided to get some bottle for the up, were waiting, it was off, again, the new crew like the others were at the front of it, fired up and wind-milling like hell, they were loving it, it lasted over five minutes, this in terms of football hooliganism is a long time, all around the car and coach park running battles taking place and to be honest, no one came out on top, Barnsley put up a great fight that day, they had to, they were on home turf, but the crew was on its debut and wanted to prove a point, with the previously told stories and on full view to all and sundry, they let no one down and scored a good point.

All on the way home and at the pub that night, the stories were flying and you know what, I bet some of them girlfriends got the best shag of their lives that night, fuck the agony aunts, counsellors and clinics, get fucking real, ale up, have a laugh, kick the fuck out of some twat not from your neck of the woods and bang crash wallop, the best recipe for sex ever.....

Over the years faces came and went and things got more organised, these times from the late seventies were aggressive, regardless of football, a fight is what most people wanted or got. We well known round Huddersfield and a thorn in most publicans' eyes, we had the usual tribe rivalry and battles.

Almondbury were our most adversaries in the earlier years and of course on our first outings into the big town we had the Legends and Myths, these stories were of the hard men of the town and two come to mind. Jimmy Johnson was the biggest name in my mid to late teens who everyone had heard of, the word was that Jimmy was the cock of the town in his days at Leeds road, he played pro for Fartown and was a bouncer, he worked the night club "Top of the Town", the rumour and myth was that Jimmy had no nerve ends, this was attributed to years of brawling and that if hit full force in the face, he would not flinch. He was a great lad and used to laugh when we were waiting outside in the queue to get in, any bother you Golcar lot and you'll know about it, he'd kick you out and anyone who has been thrown down them steep steps of that night club will remember, it fucking hurt. Jimmy was ok though and usually let us back in the week after.

I once saw Jimmy being hit with a plank of wood across the head, he didn't flinch, he took the plank off the lad and whacked and sparked him and said, that's the way you do it son.

We then also had another hard man from our era that followed us through the years, I have forgotten how many fights this lad has had with the football lads and Golcar lads, his name was Graham Swales, or better known as Swaz, he also was a pro rugby lad and a bouncer at the Golden Girl night club, I have seen upwards of a dozen lads kicking the living daylights out of this lad, only for him to get off the floor, smile and say "you can't fucking hurt me", both these lads were of the same calibre and earn the right of a mention as they were part and parcel of growing up around these times, everyone knew them and both are great lads. Swaz is now running a pub and I often pop in for a beer, I laugh at the thought of anyone causing a bit in that pub, it's the typical sort of pub though that you would expect him to be running. A good teatime working trade set of lads and always busy at the weekend. It's handy if you have a problem in the house as you have all the trades under the sun and the best two plasterers in the country in Dave Buck and Nige Kay, brilliant job for me lads, although you need to start watching Town instead of that Man U crap. When I asked Swaz if it was ok to mention him, he laughed and said, no problem Tel, I have nothing to hide and it's ok by me, as long as I get a signed copy.

This was just the start of it, in those days all the village tribes would descend on the town for the weekend jaunt, we were no different and I suppose it's just the same now but without the guns and knifes although saying that I recall around this time one Saturday night. Ellis and me were walking on Cross Church Street, we saw Irish and Icky arguing with a small group of Asian lads, we walked over and I saw that one of these lads pulls a blade. That was the first instance ever I had come across this type of thing and I shit myself. Irish is just managing to stay away from it and Icky has ripped a bin off the lamppost. He threw this with some real venom and it just bounced off this geezer's head, I could have laughed but for the point of this mad twat with the blade hell bent on doing one of us. I had seen on telly how to help disarm a person with a weapon, one way was to distract them by spitting at their face, natural instinct is to turn away and then you disarm them. So here I am, trying to do this and this bloke with the knife is getting madder and trying to get me, Irish is getting pissed off with me in the way, trying this stupid stunt and Icky is looking for another bin. The law arrives and the bastards try and arrest Irish for causing a disturbance and they wonder why some people have a racist attitude and condemnation against the police.

It was not long before we got a name and we usually ended up fighting every week. Through the years we have had our ups and downs as I have stated with Almondbury, but when the chips have been down, there was never any hesitation if a hand was needed, either down town or at the matches.

On one occasion which comes to mind, a few of the lads had been jumping taxis at a rank just round the corner from the Golden Girl night-club, this night around nine of them from Golcar walked into the rank, which was like a cabin at the top of some stairs. Knighty was ordering the taxi when the girl behind the desk disappeared, a drunken couple were ushered out of the cabin by another man and another had just locked the door, "alarm bells are ringing", all the drivers now ascend into the cabin, this one starts telling Knighty that he and the Golcar lads have been jumping taxis, "fuck off" says Knighty and with that the fella smacks him in the face with a shovel.

It's off, slightly outnumbered and pissed Golcar hold their own, it's a good old fashioned punch up with Lowey throwing a boiling cup of oxo in one of the taxi man's face and Pabs earning the nick name of "Charlie Magri" with his boxing exploits, the next thing is a few of the Almondbury lads have seen what's happening and have no hesitation, they kick the door in and they steamed in with the Golcar. Another time was when Bradford had come over to the Albion. A gig was on and it was a skinhead and punk type of do. These Bradford lot were known to Hammy, Butch and Gaz Dawson who were their counterparts from Huddersfield. A battle had erupted and a few of our lot had taken a beating. Me, Rick and the Gouch met up with this lot at the entrance of the bus station, we had a little dabble with them but the law was there. Rick says Tel Boy go and see who's in the Wellington and we will have this lot. I saw Patty and a few of the boys and told them that around thirty Bradford were giving it to the lads, on the way out of the pub one of the Almondbury lads saw what was happening and they came up without being asked or with any hesitation. We met the rest of the lads in the bus station entrance, we charged in and this lot was at the far end, Rick, grinning from ear to ear when he saw the crew arrive led the charge and a nice little battle erupted that ended with Rick and a couple more being arrested, good one on the Ambry lads but that's just what Huddersfield are like.

Willy was a right one alright; I could write a book just about him and me, like I said we were like brothers and did everything together. He was always trying to make an easy buck and I remember the time we went down to Pompey, we had a good crew and his idea was to make up lots of bacon butties because of the early off and sell them on the way down. We had cooked these at Mark's before we set off and put them in foil

We had the usual amount of ale and half the lads were still hung over from the Friday night booze up. On the bus on the way down, Willy shouts up, bacon butties lads, the price of a can of beer, we got some right piss taken out of us, someone then threw the buttie back at us and the next thing you know it becomes a war zone of flying bacon butties everywhere. We reach Pompey and find a boozer that was somewhere near the front, can't remember the name but it was a biggish pub and gradually it a started filling up with their lot. We have just under an hour before kick off and all is well, or so we think, we are just ready to leave and we have a right old reception committee waiting, it's roughly the same numbers and it's off, these lads are more than game and I think it's because of their first outing up at our end earlier in the year where a few of there lads took a pasting. Around fifty of them had come up to Huddersfield and one of these lads that looked like he was one of their top boys was a skinhead chap in a brownish boiler suit with docs. He was a dead double of action man with his haircut and was given the name action yob from the crowd who sang this to him all through the match. Like I said, this lot do not give an inch and the battle is now at full throttle with all the lads spilling out of the pub, they still keep coming and it's getting a bit hectic, it's full blown toe to toe slugging and even when the law gets a grip, they still want it. Usually in these days, like or hate them, when the law turned up things usually died off and respect in a funny way was held for them, but this lot were having none of it and credit where it's due.

The law moves us quickly and we are ushered back to the bus and we are on our way to the ground. We get inside and it's full of blue and white, I see Syko and Locky, "it's full of their boys" they say.

The next minute I see that lunging kick of Mark's and it's off again, I get twatted from the back, I remember being on the floor, the boots are bouncing off me, the next thing I know is that I am getting dragged on the floor, my fucking saviour again, Syko has me by the scruff of the neck dragging me away, it's not the only time he has had to save me and he must have been my guardian angel over the years. We put a decent show on for them and hold our own, the law moves in and Rick gets thrown out with another few lads. We are moved over to the pylon corner on the left looking towards the pitch.

What I certainly remember about this lot was it was like a scene from that film the Village of the Dammed, these fucking lot all looked the same and were all wearing the same gear, the place was quite eerie and had one of those funny feelings about it. This was the beginning of the eighties and this lot were all skins, they must have been the six fifty seven crew or defiantly the start of that lot. The next season they came back at us with a right crew

Terence OHagan

and a half, full marks to them, it was running battles all day with them, inside and outside our ground, quite a few of our lads got nicked that day. A sight that will also never leave me from that particular match was one of the Golcar lads who came down with us. He was called MT and on the verge of becoming a pro rugby star. He is of half cast origin and was well known for taking his top and shirt off when any bother was starting. He is a bit of a poser and thinks he's god's gift to the women, anyway he normally doesn't frequent the matches and it kicks off big style with Pompey. It's next to the shed in the terracing and the crew is pouring in to the ground. Pompey is swarming all over and outnumber us with half the lads yet waiting to come into the ground. They are using their numbers well and toe to toe slugging is going on all around. I look around and see MT with a group of three wanting to beat him to a pulp. MT is bobbing about taking his top off. Now whether he thought they wanted to look at his body while scrapping or he thought he was the hulk and they would run off I do not know, but you have to give him full marks for effort and cheek in the face of this situation. MT got pulled that night in the train station. We had heard that some of this crew were catching the last train down, don't know who the group were but when we arrived at the station for a gander they were a game set.

Willy laughs when recalling these episodes and tells me his favourite one is when we went to York. "We had gone on the train and around eight of us had escaped from the main body of lads, which was being shadowed by the law.

"We managed to get into a boozer and we started playing dominoes against these old fellas. Robbed us

- 38 -

blind they did. "We then went walkabout and visited plenty of pubs and the ale and day was getting better. We started making our way to the ground and saw this shop, which printed Tee Shirts. We went into the shop and saw that it was full of skinheads behind the counter. Max asked for a Tee Shirt with Huddersfield to be printed on it, they were being funny and clever so Max kicked the counter over and these skinheads with a little help from us scattered into the back room. Then some little sod (with a nod of his head in my direction !) went and kicked over all these scooters and bikes outside the shop, I remember one going over and then it fell into the next one and so on like a pack of dominos. I think everyone who left that shop had a few spare teeshirts, but we didn't get our name and Huddersfield on them. York has never been a place for what you would describe a "brawler", more of a good booze up day. However this particular outing we encounter a few skirmishes just outside and in the ground. We then noticed that a small mob of lads who we found out to be squaddie's were up for a bit of a brawl and were taunting us just outside the ground. They were pointing to the wall and beckoning us out through this red hatch in the ground wall. They were right, by the side of the wall was a hatch and after beckoning us out we piled through the hatch. Naughty lads these, they didn't wait for the lot of us and started before we were ready! No hooligan etiquette at all these squaddies, anyway it did not last long before our numbers told and they did one, although they did try and put on a show for us. At some point around eight of us managed to infiltrate their end. It did not take long for them to suss us out and we were surrounded by about twenty of them. The next thing I recall is being picked up off the floor. I had been knocked out cold, good one on them, when I came to a bit more I got another slap off one of them. The coppers just laughed and told me to fuck off or have another go at them. You can't fault those days, they were brilliant and we took what ever came at us, remember that time, me you and Ellis left the match early and waited for those Halifax boy's across from the Spinners Arms. We were sat on the wall and around ten of them walked past us, they knew we were Huddersfield, as soon as they had past us, you threw that bottle in and amongst them, at first they ran when we charged them, they then realised that they only faced three and came back at us, we stood and battled it out with them, you went down and I came over to help you, then bang, I was ten foot in the air. One of the Halifax lads had come on a trial bike and knocked me over, his front tyre landing on my bollocks. We made a retreat round the corner. I couldn't walk then Syko and Locky and a few Brighouse lads appeared and thought I was Halifax. I couldn't explain what had happened and they were going to twat me, until you and Mark appeared. Fucking sore for weeks after that, but no regrets what so ever".

Chapter Five
Going Up and Going Down

Being in the lower divisions gives you the lesser opportunities of silver wear and the chance of celebrations. Into the beginning of the seventies we were in the old first division with the big boys, at the end of the seventies we were in the bottom flight, and on one occasion it looked grim on dropping into non-league. We did not have the LSD van trophies etc of the last decade, so if you are lucky enough a good cup run against one of the big teams was your cup final and the pinnacle of performance and celebrations was promotion. Our last season in the seventies saw us clinching the league as champions and boy did we celebrate as champions.

It was the last match of the season and we had Hartlepool at home. Nothing to shout about with this one, especially with none of the monkey hangers turning up and helping us to celebrate with a good old brawl. A good old turn out from the Golcar saw some twenty five plus of us turn up and we set the stall out for the day at opening time.

We went down to Leeds road and ended up behind the goal in the open end, which had some six hundred or so people at the time spaced openly.

A shout of Almondbury took the stage with the lads replying to chants of Golcar. The mood was ok and the jumping about and banging into each other was taken light-hearted enough. The enthusiasm and beer then played its part with a couple of exchanges of punches between our old adversaries and us. Four arrests were made with both Almondbury and Golcar sharing the spoils at two each. Our Kevin and Willy being the unfortunate ones. I put some of the blame from this light heartedness to the old bill as usual being heavy handed and over reacting. The rest of the match was then on edge between the two groups wondering if it would kick off again. All everyone wanted that day was to celebrate and get pissed and enjoy the day.

The final whistle blew and that was it, party time and all of Huddersfield seemed to be joining in as well. We must have hit nearly every pub on the way up to and in Huddersfield.

Early evening saw Willy and our kid joining us in the Gallery pub at the top end of the town. They soon caught up with the festivities and the Gallery atmosphere was just like New Year, Christmas and your Birthday all rolled into one, it was really kicking. The place was really getting packed and the singing was at fever pitch, I have never experienced anything like it since, people were swinging on the chandeliers and pool cues were sticking out from the ceiling. Then chairs and glasses started flying about and the place went crazy. The landlord of this big pub must have seen what was to come and had rung the police earlier. All of a sudden down from the main doorway and from the side door, Mr Plod made its usual heavy-handed entrance but this was hardly noticed in the midst of all the euphoria. I do recall a certain DC McSweeny collaring Willy and telling him to get out of town before something happened to him.

We were baton charged out of the pub and people were just darting off in every direction. I ended up down at the Wellington with who I cannot recall but ended up waking late the next morning with one hell of a hangover and relying on flashbacks from the previous evening and expressing shrieks of embarrassment and chuckles of delight.

The main group of lads had gone down to the then Albion pub, which later became the Long Island bar. They had gone upstairs and were still celebrating and messing about. A few girls then appeared and informed the lads that MT was getting a going over downstairs in the disco by the bouncers. The lads leapt into action and flew downstairs to find the landlord (who was about 7 foot tall) and his henchmen belting the shit out of MT. The lads automatically fired in and a ferocious brawl took place. There was no give up on either side and the fight spilled onto the street, at one point one of the bouncers threw Pabs over the railings into the ring road. He landed on a car bonnet that was just passing; he rolled off the bonnet and dusted himself down before flying back into them.

Even when the law started to arrive there was no let up on both sides and although some our lot were only young and a little inexperienced to this kind of fighting, the lads did not give up and gave these lot as good as what they got. A few arrests were made and the others got away. Ellis broke his leg in that one and did not get away. Over the course of the week the rest of the lads were identified and dawn raids eventually got the lot of them. One of the funniest was a copper who lived over the road from Pabs was one of the coppers on the dawn raid, he told us he got an extra half hour in bed on that one. We went down to see the lads who had been held in police custody over the weekend and the funniest moment was when Willy's Mother turned up with a jigsaw for him to pass the time away. We still laugh at this one and even Willy does but the piss taking went on for ages. Seven of the lads had holidays at Her Majesty pleasure on that one.

We were noticing towards the end of the seventies and early eighties that some of the old guard were starting to fade and as I have mentioned a new breed of lads were starting to come through. There were some good crews developing and new friends being made. The eighties were on the horizon and a sharper better and more organised show was about to descend on us.

Sometimes through our life we have sadness and tragedy and inevitably we lose someone.

On a journey to Bristol Rovers away Sonny who was driving was involved in a fatal crash on the motorway. He was a real lad and was one of the first lads that I got to know when I first started going down to watch the Town. I will never forget the sight of him and Gassy arriving in their suits, flowers in their button holes at half time at Bradford after his sister's wedding to a mass applause from the Town lads. Chris was an up for it lad who was well respected and was one of the forerunners in the setting up of the Town Travel buses for the fans.

R.I.P. Chris Sunderland one of the great Huddersfield legends.

Mid 70s in The Shed

Usual Day Out on The Hanson Coach For The Crew

Mumfies 21st

Mumfies 21st (that's me with the Leo Sayer
haircut) This was part of the crew with the
running battles against Villa at Blackpool

The Golcar on a day out at Blackpool - Late 70s

Willy, the author in union jack t-shirt, one punch and our kid.

The big fella - "Basher" with Pido

Some of the Golcar Crew

Some of the crew at Gillingham away

Lifetime ban on two Town fans

Police praise axe on hooligans

TWO convicted soccer hooligans were today banned for life from all Town home matches.

The Leeds Road club has taken the drastic step as another move towards stamping out crowd violence at its games, and was praised by police.

Both men named in the statement from the club have been convicted by Huddersfield magistrates of offences committed during the crowd violence which marred the Huddersfield v Leeds United game last October.

Pioneers

More than 60 people were arrested that day but since then the club and the police have become pioneers in a national campaign to beat the soccer thugs.

Town secretary Mr George Binns said the two men who were to be banned were Gladstone Lloyd Malcolm and Neil Bridge.

Malcolm, a 24-year-old unemployed man from Sheepridge, was convicted in court last February. He admitted two charges of offensive conduct and was said to have twice led charges of groups of up to 200 Huddersfield fans against Leeds United supporters. He was given a community service order. The second man is 23 and

dividuals. Both have been convicted of serious offences connected with matches here at Leeds Road and have also been involved in crowd disorder at Town's away games.

"This is part of our moves, which we are always taking, to attempt to prevent crowd disorder at our games. The decision was taken by the directors at a board meeting.

Police were delighted with the initiative. Chief-Insp David Black said: "We would support any positive steps to improve crowd behaviour. I think it right that people who are thinking of committing serious offences at matches should know that the club may not want them there in the future.

Positive

"It is a very positive step. The police will support the club in ensuring that the ban is implemented. I do not foresee any difficulty in making it stick."

field for gunpowder burns to his face.

Referee Mike Riley is to report the incident to the Football League.

Town vice-chairman Geoffrey Headley said the incident besmirched Town's

But he added that the Town board was proud of the way genuine fans tried to point out who threw the firework.

Mr Headley also said the incident cost Town the chance of a goal.

identify firework
hug plea to fans

Police take no chances with this fan during an incident on the pitch

12 arrested at Town match

POLICE today continued inquiries into crowd trouble which erupted during Saturday's Town v Millwall game.

players were attacked by Town fans but police said today that allegations of assault were still being investigated.

A total of 12 fans were arrested during and after the game, with four com-

Millwall supporters was reported on a train approaching Mirfield. British Transport Police halted the Huddersfield to Wakefield train for 20 minutes after the communication cord was pulled.

Town secretary Mr George Binns said today: "We deplore the behaviour of the supporters, whatever the provocation. I was satisfied that the police and our officials acted promptly in dealing with the incidents while

Top cutting, life ban against Leeds
Bottom cutting, The Silver Fox underneath the police arrested in the pitch against Millwall after his attack against the Millwall coach

Infamous Night Out at Wetherby
Where our luck eventually ran out

Examiner, Tuesday, March 5, 1985

'Violence was worse than riots' court told

A NIGHT of violence involving Huddersfield men was described by a policeman as worse than anything he had experienced in the riots in either Chapeltown or Toxteth, a court was told yesterday by prosecuting counsel.

Reporting restrictions were lifted by the presiding magistrate at Wetherby, Mr Herbert Snape, on an application by Mr Graham Parkin, defending 20 of those accused, as all but two of the group came from Huddersfield, and local people had offered to give evidence for the defence if they knew when the court hearing was to be.

Mr Robert Marshall, prosecuting, outlined events that led to the outbreak of fighting between the police and a coach party on a stag

outing last Saturday. He said the police first became involved in the afternoon when the landlord and his wife of a Knaresborough pub were abused when members of the group refused to leave at closing time.

Twenty-four men celebrating the forthcoming wedding of one of the party were escorted out of the town and went to York. Police there stopped the coach as it entered the city and turned it away.

Later the party arrived at the Fox and Grapes, on the York to Tadcaster road, and caused further trouble to the public.

They were again escorted away by police and arrived in Wetherby, visiting several pubs.

At around 10.30 the landlord of the Brunswick Hotel in High Street called the police and one man was

until April 2, on condition they do not interfere with witnesses or return to Wetherby before the hearing.

All are charged with breach of the peace and public order offences.

These men, said Mr Marshall, were not involved in the events in the town centre, but gathered outside the police station to try and secure the release of those arrested.

They were told to get on the coach and return to Huddersfield, but they attacked the coach driver to stop him leaving and at one time threatened to storm the police station.

Under police escort they were all put on the coach and driven to the Bridewell police station, Leeds.

Charges

Remanded in custody until Tuesday were Philip

- 52 -

Town fans fined £200

TWO Huddersfield Town soccer fans were each fined £200 in Manchester yesterday.

They were arrested in separate incidents while on their way back to Huddersfield after the FA Cup-tie against Northwich Victoria on November 22.

Attack after match

A HUDDERS-FIELD Town supporter appeared before Chester magistrates yesterday charged with maliciously wounding a youth after an evening match in Chester.

80's

Police arrest 76 Town supporters

By ANDREW HIRST

POLICE arrested 76 Huddersfield soccer fans after a pub was wrecked before Town's game against Wolverhampton Wanderers.

The violence came on the day trouble flared in Brighton and Portsmouth, who Town play in the final game of the season this Sunday, at the Alfred McAlpine Stadium.

Two coaches packed with Town supporters stopped at The Grapevine pub in the Ford Houses area of Wolverhampton just after 1pm on Saturday.

Wolves fans were already at the pub and fighting broke out.

Police were quickly on the scene, but the pub had already been badly damaged.

All the Town fans — who were arrested for public order offences — were later released on police bail.

It is believed the violence was captured on video and officers will study the film before deciding on further action.

No-one was seriously hurt.

Saturday's trouble comes just weeks before England stages the European championships.

Brighton's home game against York City was abandoned after 16 minutes when fans invaded the pitch and broke down both g...

And extra p...

...drafted in when Portsmouth fans protested about the club's plight in Division One's relegation zone.

● Trouble also flared on the pitch during Town's goalless draw with Wolves when Town team-mates Tom Cowan and Mark Ward tussled on the pitch. Both were booked.

● Home secretary Michael Howard is facing demands to equip the police with water cannons in the Euro '96 football championships.

Batley and Spen Tory MP Elizabeth Peacock will make the call in the Common...

Police probe football violence

AN INCIDENT room has been set up in the wake of the mass arrest of Huddersfield soccer fans. Police have today confirmed that 86 Town supporters were arrested after fights broke out and a pub was wrecked two hours before the game at Wolves on Saturday. All were later released on police bail pending further inquiries.

Football liaison officer Pc John Topham said: "Huddersfield officers are liaising with their colleagues in Wolverhampton. Video evidence is being viewed and a number of Huddersfield men have already been identified as being involved in serious public disorder and damage."

Fans stabbed as soccer makes a grim comeback

SOCCER violence is back — two weeks before the season officially starts. Three people were stabbed and a policeman's nose was broken in clashes on Saturday.

The worst scenes were in Halifax, where hooligans ran riot after the Halifax v. Huddersfield West Riding Cup-tie.

A gang of 30 Huddersfield fans scattered shoppers and fought in the streets with rival supporters. Neil Harris, 17, needed 78 stitches after being slashed down the back with a handyman's knife and kicked as he lay on the ground.

Another fan, 18-year-old Anthony Knight, was also stabbed in the back. Both youths, from Lightcliffe, near Halifax, went home after hospital treatment.

During the match which Huddersfield won 1-0, dog handler PC William Ackroyd had his

By ANDREW CHAPMAN

nose broken when he was attacked by a gang of 10 youths.

There was more violence in nearby Bradford, where a teenager was stabbed in the back before the start of the Bradford v Leeds Cup-tie. He needed 18 stitches.

Stab death after clash of fans—man arrested

AN EIGHTEEN-year-old man has been arrested and will appear in court tomorrow charged in connection with the fatal stabbing of a Bradford man.

Seventeen-year-old trainee baker Darrell Andrew Penney, of Greengates, Bradford died during street skirmishes between rival sets of Huddersfield, Bradford and Leeds football supporters in Bradford city centre on Saturday night.

Det Chief Insp John Gamble said today that 11 men had been arrested in connection with the fights.

One of the 11, an eighteen-year-old man, had been charged in connection with the death of Mr Penney and was expected to appear in court tomorrow.

Mr Gamble said several others would also be charged with serious public order offences and would appear in court at a later date.

Police have appealed for friends and associates of Mr Penney, or anyone who was in the area at the time, to contact them.

Soccer fans' knife assaults

By NEIL ATKINSON

Fan had razor at away game

A Huddersfield Town supporter who was arrested before a game in Cardiff was sent for three months' detention yesterday and another was fined £100.

▓▓▓▓▓▓▓, of Bracken Hall Road, Sheepridge, who pleaded guilty to possessing a long-handled razor at the Ninian Park ground, was sentenced to detention.

Mr John Anthony, prosecuting, said that when police approached a disturbance outside the ground on March 15, ▓▓▓▓ was seen to push something into his left sock. It turned out to be a razor and Killeen was arrested.

In court Killeen said it had been given to him by someone else who asked him to look after it.

▓▓▓▓ ▓▓▓▓▓, 20, of Woods Avenue, Marsden, pleaded not guilty to using threatening behaviour, but was found guilty and fined.

'Barged'

Two police officers said they had seen ▓▓▓▓ waving his fists about and shouting at Cardiff fans. But ▓▓▓▓ said in evidence that he was standing in a queue waiting to go into the ground when a group of Cardiff supporters barged their way through.

One produced a knife from inside his jacket and Perfitt pushed him away. He told the officers what had happened, but they

Thugs bombard police and crowd in soccer mayhem

POLICE and club officials were today counting the cost of the worst-ever soccer hooliganism at Huddersfield Town.

In a terrifying display of violence, notorious Leeds United supporters clashed with home fans and police before, during and after Saturday's derby match.

And as senior police officers condemned the fans, the match "statistics" made grim reading:

● Sixty-five fans arrested.
● More than 20 people, including three police, injured.
● Thousands of pounds' damage to the ground and parked cars.
● First-aid volunteers pelted with missiles.

The blame for most of the trouble has been laid at the feet of the thousands of Leeds fans, who were described as "hostile and atrocious" by Supt George Calligan, the man in charge of a massive police operation.

A handful of hate. Some of the weapons found at Leeds Road

Match referee Mr Robert Nixon discusses the situation with police chief Supt George Calligan

Unconscious

This morning, Supt Calligan displayed some of the missiles thrown at his men and other fans by the hooligans. They included ball-bearings, full bricks ripped from a perimeter wall, sharpened coins, seats torn from the main stand and lumps of metal.

One policeman was knocked unconscious when he was felled by a missile, and St John Ambulance man Malcolm Wilkinson was struck by a sharp coin as he went to help.

Two other policemen were hurt by missiles thrown by a hostile mob behind one goal and in the main stand. A ball of missiles was thrown on to the field, delaying the start of the second half by six minutes, and many spectators ran for cover as seats rained down on them in the stand.

A plea from the pitch by Town chairman Keith Loughbottom and Leeds director Maxwell Holmes failed to stop the trouble, which turned to destruction after the game.

Smashed

Town secretary Mr George Binns said damage at the ground included 10 broken windows, 34 wrecked stand seats and a smashed lottery kiosk. In addition the club will have to rebuild the perimeter wall along part of the ground.

Outside the ground, more than £1,000 damage was caused to seven cars parked off Red Doles Lane, and other cars were forced open and property worth hundreds of pounds stolen.

There were running battles in Leeds Road and towards the town centre, where a number of arrests were made.

Report:
Neil Atkinson
Pictures:
Julian Hughe
Bob Stanifor

Jail the guilty — director

REACTIONS to S...day's violence ra...from sadness to an...

Town manager Mick...on left the touchlin...minutes from time...ause of the violence...said: "I couldn't see...cause or concentrate...

"The scenes made...ck to the pit of my...ach."

Leeds United director M...well Holmes said a...hurds that he we...tougher sentences to...the hooligans. He...ourts must impose...sentences on the fans...

Supt George Calligan...ail was the worst we...een at Leeds Road...olice were show...th missiles and...onstantly spat u...he Leeds suppor...were extremely ho...od behaved in a dep...le manner.

"It was a wonder n...eople were not serio...ert."

Town officials met toda...scuss the problems...ecretary Mr Geo...nns said they we...ue a statement tom...w.

The match referee,...obert Nixon, would...mment after the ga...t he has submitted a...rt to the FA because...e delayed start to...cond half and the f...at police were often...e field.

Big K, Nick, Fountain, The Author with curly hair, Jimmy
fingers, Lenny and Roger

Some of the crew's top guns

Big K, Syco. Me, Willy and Milko

Big K, Max, Pabs, The Author, Joe and our Kid, celebrating after a court victory in which our kid got off with a basket of ale

Chapter Six
The Crew

The eighties were good years in terms of violence up and down the country, the team was maturing more and many new friends were being made. Some of these were the emerging lads who had started their trade in and around the same time. It's a funny situation the football game and the different types of blokes you get to know that you normally wouldn't.

The majority of lads I got to know were from council estates as was I, but that doesn't automatically make them any tougher than the lads who came from well to do families by a long chalk. Money was becoming more available with the then government in terms of the way the Iron Maiden was governing the country. I believe she really made this country a force. I certainly voted for her and she really made this country stand up again and the people of this great island be proud of themselves once again. Looking around now, most of the people I knew then have made a decent life for themselves and are doing well.

The fashion trends were changing and the Punks were with us, the music was also changing and the "Ska sound" was in. I loved the two tone effect and we all had this type of attire and remember well the day we all went down town to buy pork pie hats and the likes. Knighty thought he was the bee's knees in his trilby pork pie hat and crombie. The first match he wore it he got it caught in the railings jumping from the shed into the terracing trying to get involved in a scrap, but he couldn't believe what had happened and cried off all day on that one.

Golcar is one of the biggest villages in Huddersfield; we have in the centre itself around ten public houses and clubs with others in and around the outskirts. In the earlier days it was the Junction where we based ourselves and after a while we moved up to the Rose and Crown. Later through the eighties we then moved in to the Wheel. The landlords of each of these abodes were all great and we got on really well with them, although our reputation was beginning to put others on edge when we frequented their place. We all got on really well and helped each other out in times of need. Some of the older Golcar lads we thought resented us whilst others would proudly say Give it to them lads and let them know where you come from. We could count our numbers in the thirties on a good turn out for nights out and around fifteen to twenty for the matches.

The more we frequented the town it seemed stronger bonds and allegiances with other groups were being made and at the start to the mid eighties it was basically ourselves and new friends such as the Gouch, Nick Rawcliffe, Syko,

Fozzer (the Silver Fox), Bullet, Mr C and the Brighouse boys, silly Fountain and the likes, that were becoming like one big happy family.

You then had the other teams around, the man himself, Basher, with Patti, Donner, Milo, and Bruiser, Dave and Tatts, Knoppy and Four eyes.

You still had mobs from Ambry and the Dalton crew with GB, Gaz Dawson and Butch with all the punks and skins crew and several more other crews. Another big gun crew who were the front runners with the England matches were the Moor boys, this troop were from Crosland Moor and headed by Cally who we would occasionally meet up with at planned venues for the big offs.

These were the days of the mad vans and it was easier to travel around in these than the restrictions that were being imposed upon us at the time with the law escorting in coaches from the motorway and beer bans. It was also around this time that one or two of the lads got married, my first stag do was for Joe Verab, it was planned we go to Manchester. The Pips was the name of the club we were going to and a full coach load was easily made up.

Looking back and laughing now at the sight of fifty brawlers in jackets and trousers, I even think the Gouch had a full blown suit on with tie, to say that most people were uncomfortable in this attire was an understatement. We were asked to pay a deposit upon arrival in case of any trouble. I don't know why they had the cheek to ask that, anyway not to disappoint these Mancs we paid. It was not long before trouble flared up, some lads had started with Joe's cousin in one of these bars and a massive free for all was under way within the hour.

How we did not get thrown out I do not know, it was not long before another brawl took place and these lot were soon taken care of.

At the end of the night it was like a comedy scene from a Keystone Cops sketch, someone went up to collect the deposit money, only to be told that the money had been given out, well just at this time a group of lads were walking out and someone yelled, they've got it, no need to go into detail but unfortunate for them lads they got a beating for nothing, then someone shouted, it's not them, it's these, another group of lads, well the same applied for them, then the bouncers became a little aggressive at us, well, unfortunate for them……. Anyway by this time, the law arrived and ushered us onto the waiting bus, only for us to find out that one of the lads had had the money all of the time and had just laughed at the antics that were going on. All the local youths were at this point ganging around the bus, being hard in the police presence when one of the lads called Tats shouted "smack him Fozzer" the Fox had still been outside and all these lads giving it outside must have taken him as one of theirs as he was giving us the fingers etc, The Fox pointed to this mouthy fucker and we said yes, he gave him a lovely right hook that downed him in one, while the rest of this gang looked on in bewilderment, the Fox then calmly walked onto the bus, nice one the Silver Fox.

It was the same thing week in week out with the weekends and the majority of the time I would wake up on a Sunday morning with a house full, either that or wake up at Ricky's house, again it would be a house full. How our Mothers put up with that I do not know but they took it well and we had a great many laughs with mine and Rick's mum to the fact that we used to take them out on the booze with us. They got on great with the lads who in turn had a lot of respect for them, even to the point of sharing a reefer, well not entirely.

What had happened was that a party was on in the Rose and Crown in Golcar, all the lads were sat round one of the tables having a sneaky joint. My mother and her mate, who both were slightly worse for wear, asked one of the lads for a drag on the cigarette he was holding. To the amazement of the lads round the table my mother started smoking the reefer, they were all looking around at each other, mouths gaping and in a state of bewilderment and thought, nice one Pat.

Fountain then told Nick to spliff another one up, confidence was in abundance with my mother just helping them finish the previous one. Nick proceeds to roll up the joint when my mother shouts across the table, hey you, what do you think you're doing, I'll have none of that in this pub, I'll get the police on you, bloody druggies, all the lads by this time are laughing and also shocked at the outburst, Nick can't believe what's going on and Fountain pops up, but Pat you just smoked the last one with us. Don't you dare call me a druggie she blasts in a state of whatever she was feeling at the time, that was a Park Drive cigarette you gave me, I have never taken any sort of drug in my life, with this, Nick had to sheepishly leave the table with his tail between his legs to encores of laughter.

One of the big guns to come to town in the earlier days of the eighties was Chelsea, all the lads were buzzing at the prospect of what were the number one "Firm" in the country.

Everyone knew of the headhunters and the reputation that precedes them. We were adamant that they would not be just strolling into Town and walking all over us. The day approached and as expected they had come in early and were presiding in a boozer called the Old Hat.

This was an Irish pub and they got talking to one of the lads in there who was a regular down at the matches "mad as fuck" Mick Kenelly. Wot's yer firm like then one of the cockneys says to Mick, now whether Mick had had a skin full the night before or just was not with it, he turns round and replies, "dere not too bad, we could do width longer breaks and also a better overtime rate you know", what that firm must have thought then I do not know, the old saying of "Northern fucking monkeys" and thick as fuck comes to mind.

One of the young ones comes into our boozer and informs us that Chelsea are in the White Hart, we muster the crew and head up towards the White Hart. Just before the pub, across the road, out shopping with the wife and kids, is Paul Clavin, what's going down he says, Chelsea we tell him, carry on love he says, I won't be long. Paul then proceeded to lead the charge into the pub and was the first to make contact, it was a shortish brawl the law were shadowing these lot and apart from a few punches and glass and buffet throwing, it was over before it got really started. We had a good team out that day and it was not long before we met up with this lot again, the word came about that they were round by the church park, around thirty of us went streaming round the corner on Church Street. I have never stopped so fast in my life and so did everyone else, we were greeted by the Chelsea firm who where all spread across the road bobbing about. All of a sudden a voice was raised and a chant of ooh ooh ooh went up, the rest responded with the same chant, it was deafening.

By this time we were all backing off looking around at each other, another twenty or so lads had by this time turned up to swell our ranks and the shouts of stand Huddersfield, stand could be heard. The Chelsea chants were now becoming quicker and they then broke into a trot followed by a swarming. These fuckers were by then only fifteen yards away and they seemed to be getting fucking bigger as well. That was it, our ranks broke and we were off, it was every man for himself. No one got slapped badly and a few of the big guns fired in but it was a tactical retreat and we laughed about this years after. It was an education in itself though and those boys had the psychological effect off to a tee.

It was not long before we met up again, we were down at a club just off the Leeds road and near the ground, just as we were leaving, and the roar went up, Chelsea had spotted us and were fanning out and coming at us, the lads were piling out of the doorway and we charged at them, we outnumbered them at least two or three to one, they did not let up and came at us, respect where it's due for their courage but our numbers paid dividends and we laid into them, no weapons just good old fashioned punches and boots, they held their line and even had the audacity to try and charge us again, by this time a few bodies were lying about and people were getting up off the floor and charging back in, it was really raw violence that both sides wanted. One copper arrived to see the onslaught and tried in vain to stop the brawl, he was chased down the road and told to "fuck off", the law then arrived in some force and tried several times to stop the brawl but because of the amount of numbers and the determination of this firm, the running battle stayed on for about another five minutes and each time both sets of firms were going for it with no back down.

While some of the lads were waiting to get into the ground, Basher and the lads saw another mob. No one recognised them and one of the lads went over and found out that this lot was from Leeds. That also then changed the mood again. This mob had come over for the off with Chelsea and the bloody cheek was when they said we've come to give you a hand. Were all Yorkshire and that sort of crap? The mood changes again, not only have we Chelsea to contend with we now have another mob who want to give us a hand and its only our arch enemy from up the road, fuck that, were big enough to look after ourselves. It was not long before it kicks off with these lot as well. Order again was restored and then inside the ground, we ended up brawling throughout the match with this lot, it was toe to toe and never seemed to stop. Chelsea after the match as you would expect, were also up for another off and came back at us on the corner of Leeds road. We had all on between the two different groups, which we did oblige, it was one of those days that sticks in your mind and you never forget which our kid won't, he got nicked for throwing a copper over his shoulder thinking it was one of the Leeds crew.

Nick later said it could have been Fat Stan and his boys who were in the documentary on police infiltration of the Chelsea, anyway, we made sure they knew that we were not a little walkover town.

Chapter Seven

Learning Curves and The Sweeny

It's not always plain sailing and battle victories in this game and the first recollection I have on what I call learning a lesson was the day we went to Preston in a cup match. We had seen this lot before and they were known to have a decent crew that would be up for it. Everyone as usual was buoyant and we took a good crew from Golcar over there. The beer was consumed over at Huddersfield and on the mini coach over to the match. We had that day with the Golcar lads, an old boy by the name of Malcolm X. Now Malcolm was a few years older than we were, a few of the lads knew him from where they worked and from the Prospect pub at Longwood we used to frequent. On the way over we listened to stories of old about Huddersfield's original skinhead gang and so on. Mally was supposed to of done a bit in his time and we were pleased to have him along with us. We arrived at Preston and parked up by the park just over the road from the away end. Town had taken quite a few over and the open end was pretty full. The song was in full swing and everyone was having a good laugh. Come half time half the away end just sat down on the terracing, in these days of old, the following in the terracing area was eighty five to ninety percent lads, the decent supporters usually went in the stands. I can remember talking to one of the lads when all of a sudden mass panic spread through the ranks, it was a mass scramble and people were climbing over one another to reach safety and come to terms with what the hell was happening. Preston had gathered their crew at one end of the away end, now whether these boys were there from the start and slowly built up or whether they had done a shifty at half time and had got in, I do not know, but they had charged the lot of us whilst we were all sat down. They were firing in to the lads with such a force that panic just spread and it was mayhem. We were all bungled up to one end and as soon as everyone got their bearings and realised what was happening the lads with no further to run and backtrack faced their oppressors and started to fire back into them. They were led by a very handy looking half cast lad in a sheepskin coat and another black lad and I would guess they were a few years older than us but that did not stop them from their goal of crushing the enemy. Through all of this and the panic, I can remember looking at these lot and in the middle was Mally, reading his match programme as though nothing was happening and when we eventually got ourselves together and fought back I looked back and there was Mally again, stood in the same place reading his match programme. I was not the only one to see this and the talking point afterwards was that this supposedly "hard lad" from a few years ago was more like a statue than front-liner. The two lessons and learning taken from that episode was not to let your defences down and never take anyone for granted, stick with who you know. Preston came back through mid week and amends were made. Before the match we popped into the Wagon and Horses. The black guy was in with a few of his mates. It was nearing kick off and we were even numbers, I was with Mick Joyce and a couple of other lads, it kicked off inside and escalated to the outside. I remember Mick throwing a bottle at the black lad, who out of nowhere pulled it from fresh air as quick as anything I have ever seen and threw it back at Mick like lightning. They came at us and we replied with the same.

I remember taking one in the mouth and Mick flying in with a great headbutt into this lad, a few more town lads joined in and a good little ruck took place, I give this lot their due, they stood firm and tight and matched us punch for punch. It was not long before the law was about and we soon dispersed. After the match, giving Preston their due, they came from the open end and made their way up to Leeds road by the old toilets sharpish looking for the off. We met them at the same time. The half cast lad (again in his sheepskin) was at the front of them bobbing about and giving it large. GPO came from the back of him and took him down; shoving his fingers up this chap's nostrils and pulling him backward to the floor where he was instantly smothered. They put up a decent fight and it only stopped when the law intervened again. The biggest lesson from the early days for me and it's a laugh that always pops up is when we visited Tranmere away. We had got there early and around twelve of us had been in this boozer. A good day's drinking was had and we were making our way back to the ground. We were nearing a fish and chip shop and all of a sudden the lads ran like hell into the shop. I thought they were all trying to get in there first for something to eat. What I had not realised was that a mob of there boys had charged us and the next I knew was that I was getting battered more than the fish, all over the place I was, the lads managed to get hold of me and the law turned up pretty sharpish. The lesson here my friends is keep away from fucking fish and chip shops and keep your fucking eyes open. It was around this time that I bought my first car, it was a Morris Austin and I thought it was the bee's knees. I thought I was Jack the lad and a lady killer with this and it made me realise just how mobile, free and great my life could be. Although I did not go to the matches in the car it made me think of other people who did and one episode in particular. Preston through these years was a regular fixture and even now it makes me laugh when I think back to this episode. Not many of us had cars and those of us who did, did not always use them for travelling away. You were tied in case you wanted a beer and also it left you and four others open with the parking etc. One particular person who springs to mind who used to use his car often was a certain person with a white Triumph. Now this fella was a good lad who loved a fight and was not afraid to get involved. This incident again happened at Preston in a league match. We had just arrived there and we were by the park crossing the road, our kid, Big K and a few of the others had gone hunting.

All of a sudden I turned and saw a bunch of Preston running towards us, they were being chased by our lot who were just managing to thump them as they were running. Big K brought one down in front of me with a rugby type tackle that JPR. Williams would have been proud of and before I could kick the twat, the white Triumph pulled onto the pavement and the occupants had jumped out to twat this lad and his mates before I knew what was going on.

My first impression was that it was the old bill and we were done for. Before I could say thanks, the lads had gone with the car as fast as they had turned up.

The Sweeny struck again in Blackpool, this time it was GPO who had an unwanted non-paying passenger, the twat tried to put his windscreen through and the lad ended up on his bonnet, still not deterred at this, he still tried to put it through and GPO driving like he was Stirling Moss to shake this idiot off ended up putting him through some railings. Another Sweeny type method from some of the lads, especially a ginger haired Moor lad and his mates was to travel in the car around before and after the match with fast surprise hits, but only with groups of the same numbers and our own sort who wanted it and this worked a treat for several years.

Chapter Eight
Around the World in 80 Days

It was around this time that I lost my job at Longwood Finishing, the reason was that I had phoned in sick and had bunked off for a mid week match to Brighton. I missed the next day and when I went back in the day after that they sent me home as they had made me redundant. Being the bright spark I was I spoke with the union and found out they had acted wrongly and settled out of court for £800. It lasted a good few weeks. Me and Willy who was also out of work then decided to set up our own window cleaning business and earn a few bob. We sorted out a round which included a couple of pubs and off we went. On the first day we had these houses next to the main road, these were three storey blocks and Willy said to me, you will have to do the top ones, as I am scared of heights! We knocked on the door and this young woman came, yes please she says, can you do them all. Anyway, I climb the ladder and starts to clean the top window which

I noticed was normal, clear and see through, this window is the bathroom window, it was not probably frosted with it being three storeys and no one could see in. The next minute the young lass walks in with just a short towel round her, smiles at me and waves and proceeds to wash her hair, Willy! Willy! I cry, she's in the buff washing her hair, fucking get down he says, so off I go and Willy shoots up the ladder, smiling back down at me. What she must have thought I do not know, one minute it was me and the next it was Willy at the window, which must have taken us at least ten minutes to clean and so much for Willy's so called fear of heights. We ended up giving it up in the end; we were drinking all the profits in the pub in the afternoon.

Life in itself was not that bad and whilst in the pub with Willy spending our day's wage, I came up with the idea of working our way round Europe and after several more beers we got really excited and decided that we could even work around the world.

Our planning as usual was left to the last minute and basically this meant packing our bags the day before we left. As it was we decided to travel to France / Germany for the grape season and onto Spain for the oranges and whatever. We also planned to go to Italy and onto Switzerland.

A big leaving party was held and all the lads came, it was the usual do at our house with a big leaving cake that Sammy's mum made for us. We got up on the Saturday morning, back packs and ferry tickets at the ready and an almighty headache with £400 in our pockets each. We got the National bus down to Victoria and slept all the way. Once in Dover we had to wait longer for the ferry as they decided to have a strike. It was a good idea at the time and we both had no regrets leaving Huddersfield and needed the break from the maddening world we lived in. The town on a weekend was still potty and with the likes of Swaz in those days walking round town with a teddy bear, just like the toff in Brideshead Revisited. He would get a beer for himself and ask whichever landlord for a drink for the bear, a great laugh but this lad was not joking, he wanted a drink for the bear and the bear was paying, you can imagine the look on people's faces and anyone he caught laughing at him would end up getting one, so you see, the break away was perfect.

Ten hours later and we were on our way. The seas were rough and Willy spent the next couple of hours dying, I on the other hand had started on the drink. We arrived at Calais and walked our way into the village centre. Nothing was open and we set about looking for our place of rest. We ended up sleeping in the only bus shelter we could find, we got the sleeping bags out and the next I knew was us both waking in the morning to birds singing and beautiful sunshine. Yes this is the life we both thought, the beginning to our new future. After ten minutes of walking round we found a café bar, no bacon and eggs and a cup of steaming tea here. We settled to shaking everyone's hand in the café and who ever else came in and enjoyed our breakfast of croissants and a bottle of beer.

It was then off to Lille which we had decided to hitchhike our way because that's what backpackers do. Five miles later and taking into consideration it was Sunday and in the country only a couple of cars had passed and they must have thought, no way. We then decided to walk a while

We eventually made our way to Lillie and were well knackard with walking through miles and miles of cornfields. We did not do that badly with the lifts and things were looking up. We spent the night in a train yard and woke the next morning under an old carriage with half a dozen French train yard workers looking at us very bemused. I was awake first and started to call Willy to wake, what the fuck this lot want he yelled, the workers then suddenly realised that we were English and I understood the lingo of "les englis" swilling there fingers around by there heads, in other words mad English, with this they just walked off. At one point in a dodgy bar, we were getting the evil eye off a few people, then this geezer notices our Willy's spider boots and we think he asks are we Legionnaires' We have difficulty in understanding and just nod, best nod I ever gave, they started buying us both beers and singing songs which we did not understand.

We decided to see what Paris could offer and made our way down there, it was an experience to say the least especially when we got kicked off the train just outside the middle of nowhere when we refused to pay more fare. What we had not known was that on some trains you had to pay a supplement of some description, after an argument with the ticket collector who we thought was trying to rip us off because we were English; we got hustled off the train. We met loads of travellers in Paris and to cut a long story short, we were told that work could be found in the Champagne Ardennes area on the white grapes, it was too early for the red grape season in the south. We then ended up in Metz where we had an altercation with the local constabulary. While thumbing to get on the motorway we noticed a police car had clocked us twice and we were getting the once over. The next thing it was like an episode from the Sweeny, a couple of cop cars screeched round us and they were out like hell. We were asked who we were and after it was apparent that we were English we were asked to show ID. Our Willy reached for his passport in his rucksack and two guns were out like a shot. There was a lot of shouting and panic, "don't fucking move I was screaming at him, just don't fucking move. We were bungled into the car and down to the station, just like in dear old blighty. After a night in the cells that saved us paying for accommodation and a free breakfast was thrown in of some description we were let free. What had transpired was that two other English backpackers had been up to no good robbing and we were in the wrong place at the wrong time. A very scary moment and I will never forget our Willy leaning over and the look on his face when the guns came out. We were having no luck and ended up in Nancy after meeting with some other Canadian backpackers and decided to treat ourselves and stay in the Y.M.C.A or the equivalent over there. We were knocked backed because we had no card from England and just walked around. We were near a building site and thought we would make this our camp for the night with some wine. We had noticed a gang of the local youths around and they had copped us. We had been in this game long enough to know when you were getting the once over and we were on our toes at the ready. We had noticed that they had followed us in some fashion when we went to buy the wine. We made our way around and noticed that they numbered around twenty.

It was obvious they thought we were an easy target and possibly had money and other things to steal and rob. After about half an hour we lost them and ended up back at the building site and settled down. Willy then hushed me, we stood against the wall and heard voices, it was the same lot looking around. They walked straight past us, we were both tooled up and ready. In cases like this you have to be, this lot were not giving up and by this time had walked a few hundred metres past us. We both agreed the best plan was to try for a Hotel or something and fuck the cost, we valued our life and did not want to end up dead or battered in our sleep. No luck with work and we headed off to Strasbourg in search after another chat with other backpackers, we then ended up in Germany. We were in Frankfurt with no money and had to call for help from the consulate. My mother helped us out and we were told it would only cost us £30 with the "Holiday Bus" all the way home. We had to endure one more night sleeping rough, but where do you find somewhere in the middle of a busy city. We were walking around and must have looked a sight, unshaven, starving and we had not bathed for three days, this tramp even followed us around for a while, in the end we slept on a school flat roof once we had shaken the tramp. All in all it was a brilliant adventure and if we had planned it out better and had been better prepared we would have made a better go of it. The best laugh of it all was when we had a walk around Frankfurt waiting for a reply on when the money was being wired over, we ended up in the red light area. We ventured into a cinema foray and had all these chaps winking at us, it was only a queers place and when I saw the still photos I couldn't fucking believe it, Willy I shouts, I know he shouts back laughing, have you seen what the fuckers do the dirty bastards!

Back home and again on English soil, we got the piss somewhat taken out of us but at least we gave it a go and found it a laughable experience. My 21st was beckoning and as usual my mother decided a big party was on the cards.

The Conservative Club was booked and everyone I knew was invited. I had family from up and down the country staying and the only downside was Town was playing away at Reading and that I would not be able to make it.

We started the ball rolling from dinnertime on that Saturday with drink in abundance. My mother made me wear a jacket and tie and off we went. It was a good mixture of age and again, the lads did me proud on the turn out. Our next door neighbours were Phyllis and Frank and were just coming to the doorway of the club, Phyllis had just said to Frank, I hope there's not any trouble Frank for Terry, don't be daft he says. At that moment in time the mad van just pulled into the car park on two wheels and came to a sudden halt, the back doors flew open and about fifty empty beer cans along with Junkie all fell onto the car park floor. The lads had just returned from Reading all beered up and in a good mood. Oh shit said Frank. Trophies from a good ruck had been brought for me as a 21st birthday gift and to everyone's amazement, they grabbed me up onto the stage to present me with my gifts. The microphone was then pinched from the DJ and the lads gave a rendition of "Wise Men Sing".

All went well and most of the oldies were disappearing at the end of the night, a whip round was had with a rather large amount of money for beers to be had at an arranged party.

How it started I do not know, but a combination of two little warring fraction groups and the beer for the party strangely disappearing, a fight then broke out. This escalated and before long the law arrived.

Two black marias turned up and several cars and dog vans, I recall the police charging onto the dance floor and one of my very close mates ran over and shouted, who the fuck invited you lot and in the process gave him a right hander. Well, that really started it off and a little tussle was had with Mr Plod and his mates.

Several arrests were made, including our Kid and Willy and a good do was had by all. It was the talking point for weeks in Golcar and every time you went into a pub, you could see them whispering and pointing, fuck em! The club gave me a life ban and refused to give me back my deposit as well. The worst was in the morning, my mother when I got in for breakfast said I owed my Uncle Gerald an apology, for what I inquired, this he says with a massive shiner, I'd only belted him when he had tried to get hold of me, the shame and embarrassment on that one, I still get digged for that even now.

There's nothing like a good away day to forget about little things like that and we have had countless of these and one episode that comes to mind was the day we went down to Charlton Athletic.

We had for that day a lad called Paul Clavin who was to drive us there, now Paul was a well known face in Huddersfield, not so much your usual football hooligan but a lively lad that loved a fight all the same, he drifted every now and then into a few games just for the fun of it when a turn out was needed. He also loved to drive cars and always thought he was fucking Stirling Moss even if it was only a pram he was pushing, however, not to mention any more into it, but some of Britain's finest police drivers have had difficulty in shall we say catching Paul…. On the road we were, a good crew, downing a few beers and what ever else in the way of illegal substances we had, a meet was planned with a few of the other crews in a boozer a short distance from the ground.

To make sure we got there on time, Paul as usual made sure every other fucking car got out of the way, to the extent that we went up the wrong carriage way in the Blackwall tunnel! One of the lads said Paul, why are all these cars flashing their lights and sounding off their horns, darting out of our way, fuck'em he says, have you seen the queue on that other carriageway!

Nothing kicked off outside the ground, but once inside, in that big open terrace of theirs a mob was eyeing the other lads up, like a pincer movement, we came at them totally unaware and attacked them from both flanks, it did not last long, most of these cockney lads have not got the balls when it comes to same numbers, although in the melee, it transpired that Paul, our ace driver had nearly been nicked and the lads made him hide in the crowd. It was a good day there and one other point of note was Basher, he had arrived and was wearing steel toe caps, can't remember if he had been working that morning before the off, but the law did not like it, they made Basher take these boots off. We were now in the open end behind the goal, we had managed to sneak into this part as some of their lads were congregating for the off, not to disappoint them we made the first move once the whistle for full time went. We shouldn't really have bothered as Basher took care of it almost single handed, he had put his boots on his massive hands and had waded in, knocking the shit out of loads of them, they were off like whippets, it was a sight though, this big bloke with steel toe cap boots size twelve's on his massive hands windmilling like hell.

It was around this time that I lost my Father; he died with his illness of being a diabetic and drinking heavily. He had re-married and was living in Morecambe. I got to know of the Funeral the day before with his relatives posting me a letter. I had ventured over several times and it was a pleasure to see him and have a beer with him. It hurt my sister the most and life is what it is. Regardless of what any person has previously been like and has been missing in your life, I am a great believer in live and let live. We spent most of our young life not seeing him and my sister the most, but at the end of the day all the wrongs and hurts pass he was our Dad. Being a Liberian I always look at all aspects and cannot understand why people prolong what I call "pity fall outs" that end up with two or more adults or members of family not talking for years over triviality. You are only here once and you never know what's around the corner, these sentences I have learned myself as I have written later in this book. Life, enjoy the fucking thing.

Chapter Nine
Mad Van Days

What I like about the Christmas and New Year programmes is the away games, if not a local derby then it's a close one not too far away. We usually have a good turn out and even the married lads get an outing to vent their frustration. We had started travelling more in vans and a jaunt that comes to mind at this period was a trip to Grimsby. This was on News Year's day, and around sixteen of us made the journey in the van. A good tidy mob and the hope of a meet with some of the other crews. The journey not too far was welcome especially with the after stench of stale beer that had been consumed from the night before. The mood as usual was full of laughter and we had some of the crew's top boys in. I remember it being quite warm for this time of year with a crisp salty wind blowing. We had parked up not far from the ground and a bit of something to eat was taken at this opportunity waiting for opening time

We ended up in the Mariners pub at opening time, looking back, we all knew that this must have been their main pub and we again expected it could kick off at some time, but with this being the season of goodwill and all, we decided just to get blathered and not upset the locals. We ended up drinking at the back of the pub, which was fully open plan down a long narrow aisle stretch from the main open plan part of the pub. No one bothered us and we drank and kept popping out to the bookies. At around one thirty we had visitors, it was the younger dresses mainly from the Moor and Kenmargra squad, some twenty of them had heard we were in and came along, they were headed by the then leading figure of a bloke called Gladstone. This chap was from Granada and here on a student's visa, he became enthralled in the football scene and loved it. Again no problem and time was getting on, it was near closing time and ready for the match, a few songs had just started and Big K led a rendition of the famous "a knock kneed chicken" when of a sudden all hell let loose on us.

We had switched off and took our eye off the ball, we got sloppy, unbeknown, all our glasses had been collected and stacked at the far end of the bar, they fucking rained them down on us, glass was smashing everywhere and glasses were bouncing off us all, the bastards, one got Knighty and sliced half his face off.

I looked up from my kneeling down position behind the bar, were glasses where still smashing and glass flying all over to see Big K, Fountain, Nick and Syko and a couple of our other big guns charge down the big aisle into their mob with tables in front of them. That was the cue, we were all up and at them, sheer numbers and weapons and still glasses smashing on us drove us back down the aisle and it was mayhem. Severe hand to hand slugging and weapons and glass were flying about all over

I was on the floor with this geezer smacking me over my head with a buffet, I frantically got hold of the buffet and lashed out with my feet, it was said later that my leg movement reminded the lads of a hamster on a wheel going ten to the dozen, not for the first time in my life, Syko came to my rescue and launched this twat with one smack.

I looked up at the brawl in the middle and noticed that apart from us lot, the dressers had disappeared apart from Gladstone and a couple of others were all that was there. There was an empty no man's land and even the long bar area was unattended. Well nearly, now I might have been mistaken and my eyes were a little blurry but I honestly thought for one moment that the Silver Fox was behind this bar in the vicinity of the till, surely he wasn't, no it must have been the concussion from the buffet head banging I received that was playing tricks with my mind, well maybe….

Knighty was losing a lot of blood, the fighting by this time had come under control and was dying off, sirens were wailing, behind us was a toilet and we could not get Knighty in, Syko blew his top and kicked the door down and told the hiding young ones to fucking get out and get stuck in or he would fucking kill the lot of them, the law came in, it was a right sight and mess, we got Knighty out and knew that we would have to fight our way to the ground, we got outside and could not believe it, no fucking reception at all, they'd done one, no fucking bottle whatsoever, they'd outnumber us by three if not four to one and did not have it for the off outside. We had a few casualties that day, a couple with bad cuts and concussions, Knighty had his nose and half his face stitched back on and one of the lads had a fractured skull. A lesson learnt that day, never take your eye off the ball, and besides, the young ones, now re-named the "pringleberry runners" by Nick learnt a few values of comradeship and just because you're outnumbered and it looks bleak, never let your mates down, stick together and nine times out of ten you'll come off the better.

This came more true later on down the line when some of these same lads went up to the Scotland versus England match on their patch, a coach load went and apart from the usual Chelsea lads, and a few dozen Geordies, this was all that England took up, the lads made a very good name for themselves and held their own. Two of them ended up being nicked and ended up in Glasgow's tough barlinnie jail for that.

I have some very fond memories travelling up and down the country in these cold and packed vans. I was from the beginning the main organiser and planner for these beauties. That was until a little argument of how much money I was supposed to be making from them erupted.

I was demoted and Ricky took control of matters. His first outing was Lincoln away and he organised a Luton van. Came the Saturday morning and we all turned up and I mean all. We could have broken the world record for squeezing so many of us in. To say we were stacked like sardines is a massive understatement.

We were all picked up and after thirty seconds the driver for that day refused to go any further, we had gone round one corner and the van nearly went over, I can remember Bullit looking at me with a weary grin and saying, this didn't happen in your day Tel. Patty and some of the other lads decided to take their cars and made it easier. Ricky resigned from organising again after the piss taking and I was re-instated.

One trick we used to play to brighten the journey back in these vans was to pick up hitch-hikers. Can you imagine the look on their faces when we opened the back doors and upwards of eighteen lads on the beer and possibly battle scarred from that day with big smiles on our faces, get in and have a beer. Knighty was always the first to wind them up especially if they were students. I remember one occasion when we picked up a girl and her boyfriend. You could tell what he was thinking and he was terrified, the girl had a beer and joined in the spirit. It went quiet and Knighty popped up, don't worry love, it's not you that should be worried, it's him we fancy, I think the poor lad really shit himself after that.

We got our own back on Mr Wind up on more than one occasion. Knighty was a perverted beast at the best of times and would always have a wank mag on the long journeys. He also had a habit of getting his todger out and loved messing about with it. This particular time in London he was doing his usual with a hard on, so we stripped the rest of his clothes off and threw him out of the van into the main traffic of London and made him follow us for ages. It soon got rid of his erection.

We weren't the only lads in mad vans and we have come across several crews on our travels that have also been game lads. One story that sticks in our minds was when AJM and his boys on a visit to Bristol Rovers had a run in with a vanload of nutters. The boys had turned up at the match all a little worse for the amber nectar and Gassy had decided that they just wear their Y Fronts. The boys were getting beaten three nil and the lads decided to go and get some ale and booze it up.

To the laughter of the others and amazement of the law, they came back behind the open end and joined a group of down and outs gathered in a tunnel. The booze flowed and the cards were out and all were getting on fine. AJM then noticed that a vanload of fellas pulled up and joined the party. These lads were the rough and ready sort and the lads noticed that something was not ringing true and AJM in particular kept his eye on them. AJM noticed that things were not right, the older down and outs were a little fazed by their new company and it was also noticed that questions put over to the older outs did not ring true like some sort of code. A set up argument followed and it was off. This lot was all tooled up and they started laying into the lads. Bars, sticks and bottles were flying everywhere. A few of the lads in the match had seen it kick off and climbed over to join the brawl running down the stantions to this tunnel area. It was then even numbers and weapons within this area were gathered which then saw a running battle with bodies flying all over. The lads started getting the better with a few more reinforcements and the van that this lot turned up with was trashed. It was trashed to the point of half a dozen of the lads jumping up and down on the roof and squashing the roof in till it hit the seats. The law restored order and it was later found out this lot was renowned for travelling around in their van and jumping folk. They picked on the wrong lot that day and I won't go into detail on the outcome out of respect to AJM and his lot.

Chapter Ten
Harrogate Blues,
Fun and Games

My life was going nowhere, with the exception of the boys and a shit job; I had the chance to move on with a building firm that was working at the time in Leeds. My stepfather Ted was a driver for this lot and managed to get me a start. I was labouring on a plumber and the firm renovated Hotels for a big name chain. The job was fantastic and moved me all up and down the country. The firm paid great money and you got the full weekend off every other weekend. The last job with the Barkways ended up with me working at Harrogate on the Stray. We could have anywhere between thirty to sixty lads on the job dependent on how big or how long the job was going to be. Working away also has its great points and again the camaraderie was brilliant. We used to get up to all sorts of tricks and going out on the town was a story in itself. One particular weekend day whilst we were working merrily away I heard the tell-tale signs of trouble beckoning. The five of us who were working in the bottom flat ran outside to see shouting from some of the lads to a rather large group marching in the middle of the road. Police were everywhere and were escorting this lot on a march. It transpired that this lot were the National Front. Most of the lads that were working had by now come out of their work areas and were giving some back to this lot, who has started it off with certain monkey type noises to one of our mates. All of a sudden, one of the lads came brushing past us with a fire hose, trash the fuckers the cry went up and water flew at pace over the twenty yards or so into this group of around seventy five. Cheers and adulation from people around went up and even the law was seen to be laughing. A few of them broke free from the cordon and charged at the lads who where only too willing to exchange punches with this lot. The next I saw was tins of paint and all sorts of missiles from our works flying over in to the crowd. Order was soon restored and the policeman gave us a rather cheeky telling off. Can't bleeding go anywhere I thought to myself. It was coming up to Christmas and we decided to have a pint at dinner time to wish everyone the best before all went their separate ways. I was allocated London for my next job in the new year. We were told to have just an hour, like so many instances in this game, the hour led into three and when we all arrived back at work we all got the sack. I went up to the other Hotel where we were all staying and again lady luck was there. The manager asked me if I wanted a job at the start of the new year, Ok I said and went home for Christmas with lots of money and to have a belter of a do that year. The new year came and it found me once again on my travels back to Harrogate, what I can remember thinking to myself would this new venture bring.

The hotel was called the Dirlton and was situated on the top end of Ripon road. My job would be working as a kitchen porter.

This went rather well for several months and again, as I said before, I have a habit of coming off well and before long, I was the breakfast chef. This came about because the chef we had was a beer monster and could not get up in a morning. I had been covering for the old sod on numerous occasions and one of the girls who the manager was shagging ended up telling him after a fall out with the chef. I was given the opportunity and grasped at this. They then sent me to day school and within eight months I became the head chef.

Harrogate is a nice little place with plenty of money about, famed for its gardens and Betty's tea rooms. It is a centralised area where all the coaches stop off and has a Hotel round each corner. It is also famed for its fairs, the Toy fair, Fashion fair, Antiques fair amongst others. It generates a lot of people travelling through and you get to meet all sorts and different types of people from different countries and backgrounds. My eyes opened at this point because all I was used to was the brothership and violence around me. The environment was totally different to all of that from Huddersfield. It was totally alien to have girls as friends and not be sexually involved with. It was not long before I got our Willy a job here, working with me as a kitchen porter. His eyes opened when the fashion fair was in attendance with all the models about and the ones that stayed in our hotel. I even set it up one morning for him to deliver the early morning coffee or tea. After he had heard the tales of the models opening the door for early morning tea or coffee, and half of these never used to wear anything, he was drooling like a dog on heat. We suited him up in black and whites and of course I had to do the same just to show him the ropes of course, it was wickedly hilarious and I have never seen so many deliveries to the round that quick. Brilliant times were had and time moved on. At first we used to visit home on a regular basis, we had a habit of taking half the kitchen stock with us as well. Our mums used to laugh like hell, well what's the point of not sharing, anyway I used to control the month end stocks and nothing was ever missed. We settled down and got to know quite a few of the locals, Bob from Manchester, Foz the video man, Buffs, a local hard man and quite a few more. They thought that these two lads from Huddersfield were mad, how true these words would come shining but we were accepted for what we were. We became part of the local pool team and made newspaper headlines by winning the pool league title for the first time in its history for the Great Western. Outsiders win the league were the headlines and we had our picture taken. We had our own little group and became well respected.

The lads used to venture over every now and then for a night out and on one particular visit Willy took them out since I had to work late. Now although Harrogate is a nice quaint little town, it also has its dark side and it was not long before it had kicked off. The lads from around this area were Leeds boys, part of the so called service crew, their top boy was called M and I had seen him and this lot around but I had not had any bother or anything to do with them.

It carried on and then kicked off again at club time opening. One of the lads had been split up from the rest, he came into the hotel and informed me that they had been outnumbered and had taken a few slaps. I called this other chef who was from Norwich who reckoned he had seen a bit of action with the Norwich boys, his name was Nick and he turned out to be a game lad. We tooled up from the kitchen with an array of knifes and choppers, we ran down the Ripon road towards the centre when I saw our Willy and five of the lads including our kid back pedalling from around twenty of these service crew, with an almighty roar me and Nick charged down the road with choppers and knifes in our hands, the look on those lads' faces was brilliant, they could not believe the sight upon then, two lads in chefs uniforms armed to the teeth charging at them, they soon dispersed and our lot caught a few of them and returned the favours that had been bestowed upon them earlier. We went trawling around to see if we could pick any more of them up and extract some more revenge, one bright spark mouthed away that "M would sort this out" when the law was around. We were busy trying to smooth the law over after they were asking things like what the fuck you doing with offensive weapons and what's all this shit going on, tell him I am looking forward to it was the reply. We got away with it because we informed the law that we were coming from our sister hotel and returning up the road to the Dirlton, we just happened to get caught up in this officer… honest.

The next morning after breakfast the lads went back, me and our Will went down to the local, the Great Western, we were having a game of pool and who walked in with a posse but M and some of the lads who had been involved in the fight from the previous night. Our Will just said, if he comes for it, smack him with the pool cue, Buffs was in and he nodded to me and winked, I thought fuck it, he's having this if he comes within two yards of me. Sure enough he comes over, Look mate he says, I understand you had some bother last night, see that lad over there with the shiner, he's the lad that gave my name, I'm the one who gave him the eye for using it. Now I have no beef with you, are we having a beer or do you want to carry on from last night.

Fuck that I said, I'll buy you a beer, now I've never been a lover of the Leeds lads but when a bloke comes over and puts it on like that, you've got to give him full marks and he deserved that. Over the months, he used to pop in and have a beer and a chat, I was offered a night out with them on a stag do to Sheffield, but that would definitely have been against Huddersfield etiquette.

I ended up getting engaged out there, looking back it was more to do with the company around us and the pressure put onto the girl from her family to get married I think. She paid a visit over to Huddersfield to meet the family, by that I also mean the Golcar lads. Well her eyes told it all. Knighty drunk as usual with nothing on and the stories of the football encounters still coming through, that along with the carding and gambling. I remember her sitting there in the Junction pub looking at a paper while I played about a dozen card games, thirty lads and she never put her head above the paper. I think all ideas about marriage were soon disposed of from that day, it was not long before she was transferred to another hotel and I then had the courage to tell her it was over... by phone of course.

One morning I was awoke to be informed that all the food and televisions had been pinched in the bottom area of the Hotel, we put this down to a party of two coach loads in the night before. Later on in years, I was informed that it possibly could have been a carload of my mates who had paid me a visit late at night. It could possibly be that these lads found the Hotel empty after gaining entry through the opened door staff room and being a little tipsy, decided to play a trick on me. It could possibly be that they then realised money was to be made and then possibly decided to pinch the bloody lot! It could be, you never know, but whoever it was I would just like to say thanks for not getting me a beer on the profits, well possibly not...

When you're away from home you often think about what the lads are up to and one Saturday morning, our Willy says, Tel, Town have got Leeds at home today, fuck it let's go. I did not need to be asked again. We took two of the lads from the pub who drank with us, never been to a match in their life. The girls from the Hotel made a big banner, Harrogate Blues....

We arrived in Huddersfield by noon, parked the car behind the Royal Swan then went to meet all the lads, what a great laugh we had with the banner, but it was soon torched by Nick and Fountain and the beer was in full swing.

As in all these big matches, a massive turn out was evident, every man and his dog, it was great seeing everyone again and stories of what had been going on were flying around. The two lads, Foz and Gary were very apprehensive at the amount of lads about and a little nervous, a few jokes were going in and the lads were ribbing them, but true to life, they would look after them.

We were all in the Fritwilliam pub on the top of Leeds road, we were just leaving and the shout went up, they're here! that was it, a mass surge towards the Leeds boys, come on then went the shout and it was toe to toe stuff with the lads from both sides firing in, no one got the better, but our numbers were swelling and the Leeds lads started to retreat. At one point as they were by the garage one of the lads threw a paving block that just missed the head of one of these chaps. They were starting to take a beating and with some haste proceeded to quickly head off down Leeds road down towards the ground, a few exchanges took place and on one occasion, Knoppy ran a full twenty yards on his own into the middle of them exchanging punches everywhere.

In all of the melee, I lost Willy and the two lads, I ended up going into the terrace, as I got halfway down, one of the lads shouted they're here, I was stood next to them, this geezer just turned round and smiled at me, I butted him and the huge gap appeared, there was loads of them, they dragged me into the middle and I got a right good kicking, Big K fired into the lot of them, but by this time, the law had me and I was arrested. Proud as fuck I as was, this was the ultimate, getting arrested against the arch enemy scum.

The cells were full, days like these often are and a familiar voice was heard, it was our Willy, he'd only been arrested himself. What a laugh, it transpires that through all the melee down Leeds road, everyone got split up.

Wills took the two Harrogate lads with him, they called at a burger bar just outside the ground and were munching when a group of five Leeds boys came up for the off, Big Bruce who had spotted them shouts over to warn our Willy and he then belts the first lad and lays him out.

The two lads, Foz and Gaz had not ever seen anything like this never mind been involved and so kept out of it, Willy belted another and before he knew it he was arrested. I was in a cell thinking fucking brilliant this when I heard Willy shout out in that that familiar voice, Oh copper, you've only put me in with the lot I've just been fighting with.

After a bit of persuasion with the sergeant who I informed that I was a chef and cooking at the hotel that night, he let us out pretty quick, we arrived at the Swan wondering where the two lads were, they had stood by the car for two hours shitting themselves and enduring the questions of different mobs asking who the fuck they were! At least they laughed at this.

£250 fine was in order and that had the writing on the wall with the manager of the hotel when it appeared in the local rag, that and rumours of a certain Huddersfield lad shagging his wife. Anyway I was getting a bit homesick and thought fuck it, it's time to go back once more.

Chapter Eleven

This Town Isn't Big Enough For Both of Us.

I managed to get hold of a job with our Kevin down at the window place so all was not too bad. I soon fell into the old routine and although I had enjoyed my little stay in Harrogate it was nice to be back home again.

It was not long before I was back in the fold with the lads and Sheffield United was at our place.

Now these lads I rate in my top five best crews of all time. They are up there with the best and you are guaranteed a row with this lot home or away. They always turn up and have done over the years.

My first involvement with this lot was at Leicester Forest service station in the seventies. We seemed to meet up regularly on the motorway in these days and a set to was always on the cards. We had one coach load of us and around twelve coaches of their lot. A bit of a do happened in the toilets and most of us were on the bus. Willy, Ellis and Sonny came flying through the doors of the service station followed by around fifty of them. They were racing like hell to the coach and would have put Allan Wells to shame.

Quickly I made my way to the back of the Hanson bus and opened the exit door, Willy made the jump in one and sonny fell in half way. The Sheffield lads were trying to pull him out and I had lifted the seat off the back and was laying into them with it while the lads were trying to pull Sonny back. We got him in and set off, panic then struck when we thought Ellis was still in the car park, but we were ok, he had managed to get in the front door of the coach

Anyway, it's down the town and we are all in the Wellington pub when someone comes charging in yelling that these lot were outside the White Hart. We got round the corner and saw Basher and Ian Langford and some of the boys already firing in. As usual they had brought a good crew and they were well up for it.

The law is soon about and both groups disperse to avoid capture at such an early stage of the day.

News again comes in that these lads are down at the bottom end of the town and this lot has been battling well against anything that comes to them. We are walking round by the post office and see them again; we have even numbers and Sheffield come charging up the road. The law has been shadowing them and automatically heads straight for us lot. No confrontation but one of the plod that is there went by the name of PC McSweeny.

Now myself and quite a lot of the other lads know this fella, the word on the street was he was demoted for discrepancies in the drug squad and the report made against him from Willy's family over intimidation; well he was back on the street. He made a beeline for me and was shoving me up against the wall. Whether this chap was pissed off at the endless shenanigans of the day's trouble I do not know, but I feel he was venting his anger on me and informing me that if I did not go away I would be arrested. At this point, the Sheffield lads had charged up at us and we were trying to appease these lads with our presence, then it happened. How to this day I do not know, but PC McSweeny went feet first backwards through an arched floor level window to the amazement of his colleagues and bewilderment to some of us. The law managed to separate us and we were moved upwards towards the town. As we were coming onto the main street, we took a right turn and headed back down towards the Crescent. Who was at the bottom end by the post office but this lot again. A couple of them were brawling with one of the Moor lads, who was called Gillingham John. Big K led the charge yet again into Sheffield who still wanted to do honours with us.

We were now on the top end of Leeds road and one of the other Huddersfield mobs that had been outside the Fritwilliam pub had now entered the fray. The law was all around and who came up to me again but PC bloody McSweeny.

O'Hagan he says, this town is not big enough for the both of us, you had better go away or something is going to happen to you.

I thought he was going to pull a gun on me or something like that from a western; again he informed me that if he saw me again that day I would be nicked. Needless to say I wasn't nicked that day but fuck him. It's funny how the tables turn around isn't it. I was at my mother-in-laws 80th the other week, the DJ who I had not seen came to the bar for a drink, Hi there the voice came, haven't seen you in ages. I looked and to my surprise it was PC McSweeny, now I don't hold a grudge and the man was only doing his job at the time, but I couldn't help replying, no the last time was when you got put through the window and you had better play some decent music, as this town is not big enough for the both of us, to howls of laughter, at least he took it jokingly..

Its Mumfies birthday do and were on our way to Brighouse on the Friday night for his 21st birthday do. Now Mumfy is a thirteen stone six foot plus skinhead who is a great lad, his brother AJM has organised the Brighouse lads to put us all up for the night. I have the pleasure of staying at Junkies house and he was renowned for liking a beer or two. The evening passes great and we drink late into the night and the talk is on the day ahead. It's my first outing to Burnley and I have never come across this lot before. All the different little groups start to meet up on the way to the breakfast in which the beer is on the go from the start. We have a fifty seater booked and it's a good old crew. We are booked for the match then onto Blackpool for the night. AJM as usual has organised a good one and done the lads proud.

We get to Burnley and have no reception committee, which for the fifty top lads that were on the bus was a bit of a downer. Again after the match, tight police control again makes sure with the exception of running a few small mobs, a no go.

So it's off again and we're on our way to Blackpool. The mood is excellent and upon arriving in Blackpool we have the likes of Knighty sat on the bus roof. It's the usual scenario on these jobs after the first few pubs; the lads start petering into smaller groups. I end up with the Bullit, Peanut and Syko, the evening is getting a little late and we're heading for a boozer called the Jack of Clubs, unbeknown to us some of our lads had kicked off earlier with another mob and we turned up with the law about, it's funny in situations like this, but it must be like a homing device built in when trouble occurs, I have been in several scenarios of the same. The lads split up and somewhere down the line it kicks off, it's like a magnet, something must just jingle the mind, or maybe it's fate, who knows…. Some of the other lads turn up and we have a decent crew of around twenty five outside this gaff, there is too much police presence so we do one down the road

How it comes about I do not know, me and Cally had crossed over to the promenade to have a gypsies when all of a sudden you hear those words, come on then. Me and Cally zip up and run across to the group in the road, it's not our lot, these lot have just been run and are re-grouping, what's transpired as we were having a piss is our lot and this other lot who were from Villa, have passed each other on the same side of the road. Bingo, a few words exchanged and these lot who outnumber us ran, they are heading forward when this geezer says to me in that stupid whining brummie accent, here mate I know you're not one of us, but you can pile in with us, I look at Cally and he winked back, our lot are now walking up to the Villa and spread across the road, we can see their faces and they're bobbing around. Me and Cally are at the end flank when Cally twats one of these lot and the lads charge forward, it's a good brawl with the lads slugging it out toe to toe and one of theirs is on the ground and trying to get away, he loses his jacket in the process and the money that was left in. Unlucky for that lad he got a kicking as well.

It was not long before the law are here, but this was one of those brawls that was to last a long while. Outside of the footballing brawls this must have been one of the best. These Blackpool bobbies are well trained, they have it all the time and they deal with it unlike other town bobbies, again they maintain it's their town and would we please vacate the premises as they wade in truncheons on the go, yelling about this being their town. Both groups separate and get out of the way down the backstreets, the only trouble is that we keep meeting up again and again and again, all the time the law keep piling in, but no one gets arrested, it's toe to toe and good old fashioned swing punching. Their mob seems to get bigger every time we meet them again, it's a fine old performance from the lads and two outstanding lads of the night were Basher and Fountain, Basher as usual with his handy work and Fountain (has Poggy stated) was like a general that night, barking orders out all the time and geeing the lads on, pushing all the time and keeping morale on the go. As I said these lot were gaining in numbers every time we meet, they'd pulled blades and although no one from our side got injured with them, Syko had his jacket slashed at the back. In the end, the law are that pissed off they charge us one last time and make sure we are well and truly separated. Our kid a few years later was having one of his little holidays at Her Majesty's pleasure down near that way and these Villa boys after asking him where he was from starts going on about a mob from Huddersfield and that night in Blackpool, our kid tells him it was his brother and the lads, it was only the lad who had lost his jacket, he tells him that we put up a very good show for the numbers we had and were one of the best that they had come up against.

We get to the coach park and see some of the other lads, we find out that one of the boys called Ali had just been accosted by a group of lads, a foreign body they had called him and given him a slap. We went over to the burger bar and just remedied the situation, only trouble was it escalated and the burger bar went over as well. I was really pissed off at that, starving I was, but a good ending to the night and a big up to AJM for that one.

Chapter Twelve

Porridge and Sad Old Ray

It is inevitable that casualties will be met in terms of people getting nicked, even to the point of lads enduring Her Majesty's pleasure, over the years we have lost an odd one here and there for a while, our kid had several of these. Now the lads that I have associated with over the years have all been good lads and the only time Court has beckoned has been to do with football matches, stag parties or other related fighting incidents. I always remember Knighty saying that the lot of us will all get it together after a do like some of the crew had a few years earlier with the Albion job and not something silly on our own, we used to laugh at him over this, but how true those words came ringing through. Up and down the years we have had a few close calls and one or two of the other mobs have had it given to them and made an example of. Northampton in the late seventies, several of the lads went on a revenge mission. The previous year one of our boys lost an eye, several whom I will not name endured custodial sentences for that. Bristol Rovers away, as noted earlier, custodial sentences again. The end of season bash at the Albion. The Wharf in Huddersfield are a few to mention. Now if we had been sharp enough the law of averages would have told us that up to now, we have had a very good run, but in the mid to late eighties we as everyone else just take this as part of life. It was the environment of that decade, we were just like any other set of lads up and down the country, no different at all. When it did come, it made national headlines in both the media and papers, it was a big one and how those words of Knighty's rang through my head.

It's our Willy's sisters wedding, getting married to a lad called Pete from a village just up the road from ours,'Cowersley. He is a great lad who has also frequented our travels away a few times, this lot have a very tidy mob that are headed by big Tom and Berto, we have always been very good mates with these lads and the stag do is organised by the Gouch who is the best man.

It's a breakfast away at ten in a boozer down Bradley, again, we have a fifty seater full of the top boys, it's Knarsbourgh for the day session which passes peacefully, it's the same as any other time, breakaway little groups and each keep meeting one another in the pubs. There are one or two little fall outs at times, this in itself is not that unusual and is also part and parcel of the day, once the beer is in, it's the wits out. We head up to Harrogate but end up in Wetherby. We had called in another couple of small towns but had been moved on, we were being shadowed by the law all the time. Again it's peaceful enough and even the local yokels are having a laugh with us, around twenty or so of us are in this boozer when a little piss taking comes out, because of the amount of beer consumed that day one of the lads takes this the wrong way and a few fisticuffs start between us, this escalates outside with a bit more brawling, nothing serious and it's all broken up before it starts, we split into two groups and around a dozen of us go into the Brownlow pub.

We are all having a laugh and joke again with the rugby team that's in this pub when all of a sudden the law comes piling in, truncheons drawn, we think it's this landlord that's called them, it comes out in the wash, it's the other landlord from the pub across the road where we had a spot of bother between ourselves.

These fellas had come to take no prisoners, now don't get me wrong, each to their own and these fellas have a job to do, but as all of us know, there's a right and a wrong way on approaching things. They zone in on a dark skinned chap who I will not name, obviously because of his colour, they smash his glass out of his hand and all the time they're telling us to get out, we're trying to reason with them and that's when it kicked off, they start to club our mate in the doorway, fuck this, we pile in, I get my nose broken in an instance, I'm seeing stars here, and it's like slow motion all around, this had been a set up, we had law from all over Yorkshire here at a tiny village town ? anyway as we are trying to stop six police from battering one of the lads over a cop car, the other group have come out of another pub and see what's happening, no second thoughts are needed, it's straight in. A fair few of us by this time are covered in blood, all the time more police reinforcements are arriving, again as I have stated earlier, I do not know how it is but the rest of the other lads start turning up, by this time we are near to a full crew that started off, cop cars are getting battered, people are being dragged out of police vans and windows smashed, more police are turning up and a very large crowd have gathered to see the events, it's reported in the paper as the crowd are singing "Kill, Kill, Kill the Bill, and which even compared to nowadays was something of a first as a full blown bloodbath between the law and a set of lads, no holds barred at all. The lads fought toe to toe and slugged it out with the law who were tooled up to fuck, but as the famous lyrics from the song by the Clash state it was a case of "I fought the law and the law won".

Vastly outnumbered and the point of a dozen or so arrests sees us backing off and dispersing into the crowds which if we were chased by the law, the crowd swallowed us up and gave the law verbal hell.

We regroup near where the coach is and we have a lot of angry people, the law were way out of order and a lot of battered lads were out for revenge, it was at this point that two local lads ended up in the middle of us, now whether it was nerves and the sight of so many lads covered in blood and battered they decided to join us after asking what we were doing, Fucking storming the police station came the cry and let's get the rest of the lads out of the nick, well that was it, we got onto the coach and these two lads joined us, well up for it they were.

We arrived at the station, now in court the police informed the jury that one of the lads on the bus had driven the coach and not the actual coach driver, the driver actually said that he was the one who had driven us to the station, proceedings were stopped and the prosecution called hostile witness and that the witness had been tampered with, it was also stated that other witnesses could also have been tampered with, again nothing was ever proved and I certainly do not know anything to this…well I wouldn't say if I did know.

We arrived at the station, which had officers still about, we managed to force our way to the doorway of the police station, alarms were being sounded everywhere and Sweeny type cars were arriving at the said time at the gates, off it kicks again and a few more are nicked, it quiets down and we are shepherded to the coach, we were told to get back onto the coach and go home, now after a lot of toeing and forgoing we are escorted on to the coach and the bastards arrest us all, fallen for it again, some of the lads have seen this coming and have managed to escape.

Wetherby is full to the beams so we are informed that we are going to be processed at Leeds Bridewell nick, anyone from these parts of the woods will know that at this time this place was a fortress and hellhole. I was sat at the front seat handcuffed to this young officer who was winding me up to the hilt, how I did not crack him I will never know, he got the verbal enough though, we pulled into Bridewell and at the back is a long slope into the station, this is being filled up either side by officers tooled up to the hilt, what has come to them and the main reason we were also arrested was that eight police officers had been hospitalised and one of them was a woman officer, these fuckers were going to give it us good style, the doors open to a frenzy of very mad tooled up officers and the young buck says to them, this one's got a complaint against police brutality, that was the cue, I was dragged over the handle rail and bludgeoned to hell on the steps, I was then hurled up the tunnel of death where

I received one of the best beatings of my life and was the first to be dumped into the cells which were the old fashioned cage cell barred all round, the next lad in who I will not name kept having his head smashed against these and left a three bar mark on his face for days, Bullet was the next, he splattered against the wall and sunk down leaving a big bloody mark against the wall. We got it good style, every one of us.

Again I was the first one processed and was launched before the sergeants desk, what's your name and address, fuck you I says, I am saying nothing until I see a police doctor, with this the sergeant had leaned over and lamped me with a good right hander that knocked me flying over, the two young police bucks held me back up and said, for fuck sake give him your name, Terence O'Hagan I said, That's better little boy he says, now fucking give me your address, fuck you I replied I am not saying anything… smack I did not even complete my sentence and I was on the floor again with blood spilling everywhere..

Two fucking days we were kept in that stinking hole and when we got out we stopped at a service café on the way home, who walks out but the comedian from Barnsley Charlie Williams and asks the question of why we look why we do, Oh he says you made the bloody news you lot, anyway, well done lads…

To get to the point, twenty three of us received sentences, which ranged from three months to the station assault to four years on one of the lads a total of thirty plus years was handed out, the two local lads who joined us for fun, never got involved and came to watch, they both received three months, now there's a lesson to be learnt eh…..

It was on the cards as they say, in the end they got us and we could not cry about it. We ended up at Leeds and then at Durham.

Now I know on my part as well as other lads I know, this changed a lot in how they then decided to live their lives, there is nothing good about being in jail, I hated every minute of it, I was sick to the teeth when the judge turned round and said, Terence Owen O'Hagan, I sentence you for your part with others…. Every time I watched Ronnie Barker and heard those words at the beginning of Porridge. Norman Stanley Baker….

That for me as well as the majority of the other lads was the first and last time of our freedom being taken away from us, I could write about the things and laughs we had whilst we were in there, but I will not, as I stated, there was nothing good about it and I hope any young lads who are reading this take note of this passage…as Knighty would say, no gain without pain, commit a crime you do the time.

At the end of the day, was it worth it…. Ask those eight police twats who ended up in hospital that had themselves inflicted pain and hurt on us. One thing that also puzzled me was the amount of police officers in court who stated that they were in "fear of their life" now we were outnumbered three or four to one by the law and plus the fact that they were all tooled up, just what are our police force made of, it just makes you wonder eh.

After our release on which the inevitable was that most of us were out of work, four of us decided to pool together to start our own little underwear business. This was masterminded by Pabs who had not been sent away and three of us who had, Max, Knighty and myself.

We all chipped in £100 each and headed over the tops to Manchester market area. Several shops around here sold all the cheapest underwear and sexy lingerie. We spent every last penny on the lot. We then went back home, got a suitcase and planned our route around the pubs. It was great fun and we started making a few bob. Knighty was getting a bit fed up and we bought the moaning old git out, doubled his money in less than a week. That left the three of us and we carried on for a few more weeks, progressing onto jeans and the likes. The only problem we really had in a game like that was the scope of people we could sell to. The majority of our clientele were in pubs and of course you ended up boozing part of the profit. This sadly came to an end but all in all it was a good laugh and a great puller for the lads when we were out, like "I know what you're wearing under that skirt tonight".

Shortly after this I bumped into little Raymond Haley who was a few years older than me. This bloke is a right Arthur Daley character and loveable rogue type of bloke, he always had something to sell. He is one of these that could sell snow to an Eskimo. Anyway, Raymondo was in the pub and asked if I fancied going down Kent hop picking with him. Raymondo used to do this every year jail permitting for one reason or another. I had heard him previously going on about Kent and the hops and all the people who knew him etc and thought fuck it and decided to go with nothing to lose. I managed to get the train money from me mother and off we went, Ray who always had a story of one kind or another kept me entertained through out the journey. When we get there we have a week before it all starts and I know of these big houses on estates where we can work and so on he yaps at me.

We arrive in and it's the usual quaint type of country place, our first night of abode is some caravans that Ray has got us into, great place, all the mod cons and beautifully clean, fucking duck Tel he says, what the fuck is going on here Ray I say, that's the bloke who owns these two caravans and he doesn't know we're here, but you had a key you little twat I say, Ray just turns around and smiles. We had better not unpack until I get you in somewhere else in a few days he says. Now Ray kept to his word and found us work in these big estate houses which unsurprisingly they all knew him until the following week when the hops began and he got me on a farm where he used to work. I was glad of that, I felt I had just undergone a week on an SAS assault course with the wall jumping, hiding behind bushes etc in that borrowed caravan we first stayed in.

My first night on the farm was brilliant, I ended up in a caravan sharing with a couple from Ireland, the drink flowed and conversation was good. Off I went to bed and within half an hour or so I half woke to the caravan shaking and moving about, as my mind tried to comprehend what was happening, I am sure I heard the girl shouting Terry, Terry Terry and then a noisily scream of yes, yes was heard. Whether or not my sub conscious was playing games or within my drunken half-awaking I did not take heed of what was supposed to happen it all became clear the next day. We have a newcomer to the caravan, which then made four of us. The lad was an Australian and his name was Tim. Now Tim seemed a good lad and had been working his way around the world and he would arrive here every year at the same time as he had for the last three years. Tim was a street wise lad and after a few drinks I told him of the previous night to which he just smiled and said let's hope so.

Again after working the hops, it was tea and back on the booze, Tim and me were bunked up in the same room and after about an hour, sure enough the caravan starts to move and rock about, the next it's Tim, Tim, oh yes…. Well we just fell about laughing. Three days later Tim shacked up with this bird after she dumped poor Paddy. He had obviously got into her and that was the last of any other name-calling we heard.

Again, this was another chapter in my life where I was being educated in the way of the world. Being down in Kent was a million miles away from the violence and football that I knew. We had all sorts of people from all over the world here but the majority of workers were the travellers. Now these guys' whole existence revolved around dope and cannabis and what they could do with it was mind blowing. One of the travellers was called PeeWee and this fella was constantly stoned. After having a smoke with him, the crafty sod asked if I had the munchies to which I did, right then he said, we will have some of my favourite honey on toast and a cup of tea. After several slices from this massive jar I was getting a bit full, the rest of the group were having a bit of a giggle and around an hour later I started to get a little edgy and stupid. It was if the world had closed in and everyone was having this laughing fit, if someone spoke we all laughed, what the bastard had done was laced this jar with magic mushrooms and I was feeling the effects of this. Never trusted the guy again, although looking back I should have realised and it was a just a laugh.

PeeWee knew I was a cook and one day he decided to cook for the whole gang of hoppers, he decided on a spaghetti bolognaise to everyone's delight. Tel he says, how do you know when the spaghetti is done, when it doesn't stick to the wall was my reply winking at Tim. Tim and I went back to the caravan an hour later. He was in an apron of some description which was filthy, he had an enormous spliff which the ash was dropping into the sauce and he was constantly throwing the spaghetti at the wall and saying, not yet in his doped up presence, Tim looked at me and we decided on a take-away from the village. All in all it was a good experience and I will always look back and think of the laughs that we had.

I had got a phone call and my old place at Bradley had a job going, I was by this time also missing the excitement of the football in which the season had just got underway, I was on my way back home. A good one to Ray and whenever I hear the song from Mick Hucknel "Sad old Ray" I always chuckle.

Chapter Thirteen
Big Boys and Huddersfield Abroad

A couple of things happened to me around this mid to late period that had huge effects on the rest of my life.

On coming home I met my then first wife to be. She came from a well to do family and I must have thought that this was an escape from the messing about that I was going through. We had a quick courting period followed by our engagement. This was held at the Wheel in Golcar and again, the lads did me proud. We had a room above the pub and I do not know how it started but a fight at the end of the night began between known friends, this escalated and got a bit out of hand, knives were drawn and arrest were made. I spent that night in hospital with a friend who had to be revived several times on the trolley, he nearly died. This makes you think out aloud over things like this and I was really scared when this happened. To see someone in front of you like that nearly losing his life is very scary. Gary is ok now but our friendship over that episode became strained and I only ever saw him twice after that.

Life carried on and a big one was on its way to Leeds road. It was Millwall, one of the big boy brigade. I had seen the stories on TV about this lot and also it was still a talking point about the Luton game. All the lads had turned out for this one and we scoured the streets looking for them before the match. We had heard rumours that they were about but this turned out to be a no go. Inside the ground about twenty of us had gone to the terracing next to the open end. They had brought a decent team of around three hundred up and were making some noise. The final whistle went and a few of their boys started getting onto the pitch, not to be left out and hoping for a good row we all got onto the pitch and started running over to them, a few more from the terracing joined us. They noticed that they had company and were only too willing to take us on. Shouts from the team on hold it and don't let the cockney fuckers have us were coming through. More of their lot were getting onto the pitch and I thought fucking hell we're well outnumbered here. A big black lad led them and all of a sudden they started backing off, what the fuck's happening here. I looked around and saw a beautiful sight I will never forget, all the cowshed had seen our little charge at these lot and thought fuck it, we're having some, around three hundred lads plus shirts were tramming it down the full length of the pitch to join us, the first thirty or so lads all backed off and rounded the big black lad and stormed into the group before numbers meant that someone had to tackle him. He went down and Millwall with their so called hard reputation got smashed and well battered, it was one hell of a result that one. The only downside to the day was that The Fox got nicked. As the brawling got going he felt someone grab hold of him, he turned and laid the fella out, it was only the assistant coach of Millwall. He thought that his days were numbered and would be banned for life. Came the day he was let off rather lightly with just a £200 fine. Great result that one. We knew that the return would be met with vengeance and retribution and a team of around two hundred of us took the journey down there. The arrangement was all to meet up at Victoria station and we would go by tube into the den. We went in the mad van as usual along with several other vans and the main bout of lads travelled down on two coaches. We were all tooled up to the nines everywhere and at the service station the law pulled the coaches. One of the lads had nicked something and the law got onto the coaches to search them. All the iron bars and other objects of ill repute were stored through the top hatches on the coach. The law then got off the coach and told the drivers to take them on their way, in doing so the bars and other weapons rolled off the roof. Both coaches were taken to the nick and the lads had to stay there until the match was over, that also made the news and paper headlines. Meanwhile, somewhere in deep south London, our little van was lost, we were all tanked up and looking for Harry the Dog, we stopped at this bus stop and asked this oldish black geezer where the ground was, well he says, you can give me a lift as I am going that way. We must have travelled a few miles and the geezer who had had the piss taken out of him by eighteen pissed up lads for the last fifteen minutes says here will do, he gets out of the van, where is the ground then mate we ask, just round the corner from where you picked me up you twats and fuck you lot, off he disappears round the corner, well you have to give it to the man don't you for the nerve of it. Nothing comes of the day only for us to be kept in half an hour and when we got back to the van the windows had been smashed, what a lovely warm journey we had on the way home.

One Sunday night I am woken to find out that my dear little sister has died in a house fire, this knocked me for a six and it took me weeks to comprehend on why she had died and what a waste of a young life. All the lads knew her and as she got to the stage of going out on the town, there was always someone who would be there and keep an eye out for her. She was great friends with Ricky's sister and brother and came the day of the funeral you could not move anywhere near the church. The lads all showed their respect in a huge turn out and two were pole bearers with our Kevin and me. I certainly found out that my friends were always on hand and thank those for the help they gave that I needed in this one of my darkest hours.

R.I.P. Mandy O'Hagan never to be forgotten, will always love ya kid.

There have been countless stag parties that I have frequented. Each one has always a story to tell and there are countless, no doubt some of the lads will ask why I have not spoken or written about this one or that one, but I have written of the two from this era that are remembered well with everyone.

I'm getting married and around this time people have started having stag parties abroad, so why not I thinks, after inquiring and organising the event, we have got a weekend in Ostend.

A thirty seater is booked and the lads are rubbing their hands, it's a first do abroad for most of us all together and we're well up for the weekend ahead.

As per usual on these do's a couple have fallen out and cannot make it, we hit the town for the Friday afternoon session and the off time is 11.30p.m. from St George's square, we have a fair old team and some of Huddersfield's finest, Rick, Max, Knighty, Pabs, Nick, Fountain, Milo, Clever Trev, Muggsy, Roger big balls, Jimmy fingers, Daz Traverse, were just a few to name, we're in the last pub before the off when one of the Moor boys asks where we are going, Ostend, fuck it can I come, the only trouble is that I have only got a tenner !!!!! So Friday (called this because of his skin colour if you get the pun) joins the ranks, it turns out to be his best ever weekend and he comes back home with more money than he went with !!!!

We're on our way down south and call in a service station, no one pays for anything and the night is set with more blue smoke than anything else. Anyone who falls asleep is given a "mad monk" haircut, this is a bald patch on the crown, Jimmy Gumby is the first, very long hair this chap and his pride and joy, he could have cried, but that's the rules.

On the ferry we buy just about every pack of cans we can and the session begins, Puny spends most of the trip throwing up, it's noticed that two other groups are on the ferry, a mob from Chelsea and a very large number from Wales who were all dressed up and looked a set of dicks.

They keep well away and a few verbals are thrown at Chelsea who at the time then, laugh it off.

We're all booked in and it's time to sample the delights of Ostend red light district area, later in the afternoon we come across the Chelsea mob, it's obvious they have had a few beers and they give us the look that tells the story, it's come to light where we are from and a few of these lads look to have taken a great dislike to us. This is in reference to the Chelsea lad who died at Huddersfield after being hit on the head by a pool cue, the lad who had done this, known to some of the lads with us, had acted in self defence, the lad from Chelsea had died the following day in hospital, we could go into the ins and outs but at the end of the day a fatality is something that no one really wants.

Before they decide on what action to take, we could tell half of these lads did not want it, you can tell by the way they look away and cannot keep eye contact, we are talking loud enough so that they can here us and one of the lads throws a glass and we charge, sure enough they panic and run, a few punches are thrown but it's left at the departing mob to do one, no point in chasing this lot half the night, we'll see them back on the ferry tomorrow.

A few hours down the line and we're in the middle of the rough part, clever Trevor is having a row with a couple of the locals, we tell them to do one and fuck off to another bar. We notice that these lads who we have been having a row with turn up, with a few more in tow, it's also noticed that every few minutes a couple more would come through, now we've been in the game long enough to know what's coming here, so we think fuck it, you having it first, it kicks off, a right good old fashioned bar brawl with everything flying about, buffets and smashing glass everywhere, I had fired into two of them with someone else and ended up with my jumper over my head, swing my arms everywhere till Fountain grabs me and tells me to stop hitting fresh air and pile in with my eyes open, it spills into the street, these twats are using baseball bats and all sorts of weapons, the bastards are squeezing ammonia through washing up liquid bottles as well, Daz T runs over the road, two couples are having coffee outside, excuse me love he says, I need to borrow your table, he pulls it away and runs back over the street, he launches this at the window, only for the table to bounce back and flatten him. We are now hand to hand in the street and it's getting hectic, there is no let up, they are piling out from all the bars and their numbers are swelling, we are greatly outnumbered and it's getting grim, we're still holding it together and it's our past experience that is paying off, we're fanned out across the road and bodies are lying everywhere, then that familiar noise fills the airways, the law are here, in circumstances like this, being vastly outnumbered it would normally be a good thing, but if you have been in this situation yourselves you know what I'm going to say next, we are aliens in their country, the law piles into us with those big truncheons as well as the locals, a tactical retreat is called for, we disperse and are on our toes, lads are getting nicked and the doctor (M F) shouts Tel Boy, get into those taxis over there, I jump in one and as the doctor opens another taxi door the law gets him, he nods and winks. It's back to the hotel and several other lads start to turn up and we re-group, the law has turned up and are taking the passports of who have been nicked, the manager is here and after a lot of talking and assurances and a big bond decides to let us stay. We have a few battered and bruised lads and the decision is to go back to this part of town again. Nothing kicks off and the next morning the lads are let out of jail with a fine, all went well with the exception of Ethel who had woken up in the cell minus his underpants..... He has never really told us what happened that night...

It's off back to England on the return trip, Chelsea are nowhere in sight and the Welsh lads keep well clear after a few obscenities are thrown in their direction, after an hour and more beer, Nick ends up fighting with a kiosk attendant who thought he nicked his cigs, they closed the bars down, the lads then go on a frenzy of flushing anyone who moves, this involves throwing their beer over everyone after shaking the can up, the purser is called and tries to calm the situation down, he gets flushed and told to fuck off, he then turns up with the crew from below and stokers etc, a right handy bunch, it's all geared up but a few of the lads have still a few scruples left and they persuaded the rest not to start, we could end up being locked up for a few years on this one. The law is waiting for us at Dover, no arrests were made, some of the lads had managed to get through the blockade mingled with other passengers, these are the ones that were going to get pointed out, well it's a laugh and half way back up the motorway the law is waiting again, this time for the money that was not paid at the service station plus a bonus for the staff who we are told we mistreated, well, pay offs are better than jail!!

I was not the only one getting married and also around this time, one of our top boys who also decided to get married was the Silver Fox. This fella along with

Syko is renowned for gambling and it was odds on his stag do would be a racing trip. It's the St Ledger and it's at Doncaster. Come the day we're at the Woodman on a good old breakfast. I along with the others were hoping the omens were going to be better than the previous breakfast stag do we had here (in reference to the Wetheby stag do)

As you would expect the food and beer are in full swing and the betting and carding is already causing laughs with money changing hands at an incredible rate.

The time's come and we're off on a jaunt to Doncaster races, again it's a fifty seater full of Huddersfield's top boys, the day passes well and all are having a good do. It's the usual with half the lads not even seeing the races and staying at the boozer all the time. The races are over, we all board up, some complaining of losses and others jubilant, we call at a big boozer just the other side of the racecourse. The landlord has no problems with us and he's quite happy, all is well and the card schools are going, a few of the lads go into the eating area. One of the lads says eh up boys who's this lot, two coach loads of lads start coming in and within seconds we know they're from the Leeds area.

All is fine and a few exchanges on what should have won and what not should have won were taking place with some of the older members from this club, there's a big group of lads huddled to one side and led by a big bearded chap that start singing "who's the dick head in the hat" this is in reference of Bullit who for some reason I cannot remember had this silly hat with big hands on it or something daft like that, Bullit looks over to me with that smiling face of his and the hat is slowly taken from his head, in only a second or two, the lads who are spread out through this big boozer have eyed up ever possibility of events, it's like slow motion, we all know what's coming, a sort of telepathy has just whizzed through at supersonic speed, this lot just start to give us a rendition of that stupid song Marching all together when the first smash of a glass is heard, Burky and Mr C lead the way and it's all up and in to them, no mercy is shown, we have had countless meetings with Leeds and they always put up a good one, but I can honestly say that we have never come second best, even the time in Bridlington from what I am informed, when the young Golcar of then with a few of the experienced boys, met with a full coach load from Leeds in the coach park, that even made the news on telly, anyway the big fella with the beard is not going down, fair game to him, as at times he must have been fighting two or three at once, at one point the doctor has just finished his meal, he comes through the door and smacks this chap over the head with a bottle and he still did not go down, I remember seeing one big Leeds lad with a white teeshirt on, when I looked over again it was red, someone had brought the old cut throat razor out to play and this chap was there to prove its existence, we come out on top and before you know it, the law are here, again we are put onto the coach, the manager with the law comes onto the bus and says it's a fiver each lads for the mess and forgotten.. I have never seen so many lads empty their pockets as quick.

Chapter Fourteen
The Milk Train and Left Behind

Life has a habit of turning up the unexpected, no more whatsoever than for me and Willy. One event in particular that springs to mind is a Friday night on the town with our Willy. Nothing unusual about this and this night we decide to do a runner round the town and call at the different bars that we do not usually frequent. This involves a quick half and as many pubs as we can manage. We also decide to drink cider for some unknown reason and it's not long before the effects start to pay off. It's about ten o'clock and we were in a boozer that we usually did not go to, it's quite lively and we are standing minding our own business when this silly twat with no trousers on bumps into our Willy. We take no notice but he bumps into us again. A nice little argument breaks out with this chap's mates intervening and getting rather angry at the two of us. Rather than cause a scene and taking into account our state of mind we decide to move on to a lovely little nightclub called the Amsterdam bar. A while later in comes no trousers with his mates and guess what, he wants to play bumping into us again. This time our Willy gives him what for and we pile in, some of the lads are in and a good little brawl erupts and we sort this lot out in no time with the help of the bouncers who just happen to be friends of ours. Nothing unusual about this little occurrence you may think which looking back was a weekly thing and then forgotten about. The Saturday night Willy's cousin has invited us to a Wedding reception. We have a few beers and head off to this reception around nine. Not a bad venue and the place is well full. I go to the bar and get the beers, just at this time Willy's cousin has dragged him to meet the bride and groom. I hear a shout from Willy, Tel boy get here, I arrive and see the groom shaking hands with Willy. It's only bloody no trousers with a lovely shiner, for some reason he doesn't recall us and we think we have got away with it, the best man turns up and throws a punch at our Willy, this fucker remembers.

We make a very hasty bolt for the door followed by smashing glasses and all and sundry chasing us down the street, the last vision I had was the bride throwing a bottle at us as we ran like the wind laughing our heads off. Life's still good in Huddersfield but like I said there's always something around the corner and it's not always the good things that you remember well.

To me there is no feeling worse than coming round with the effects of the beer wearing off in a cell miles away from home. Realisation kicks in and the hope that you are not the only one that has been left in this predicament starts to buzz through your hung over head. You can guarantee that chucking out time will be around midnight when the last train from whichever godforsaken place you have the unlucky pleasure of being in will have gone.

I think the old bill have great delight in some kind of perverted and twisted way and are laughing their socks off once they throw you out of the door.

Most of the time dependent on where you are it's a case of catching the first train back home the next morning or the milk train, as it was commonly known. My first experience was Northwich Victoria away. It was an FA cup match and we arrived in this Cheshire town just before opening time. We had just come out of the station and were walking towards the village centre, a car load of lads whizzed past shouting abuse, mmm I thought, even for a little place such as this we might have a bit of fun with the locals. The day passed on with several beer holes visited and no opposition encountered. However we passed one local a little later and saw several of the lads being spread-eagled over the police cars. No opposition was to be seen and as we passed we took the piss out of the lads that by this time were being led away. I ended up with John Faye in this little boozer in the centre; the landlady there informed us we were ok for a lock in. John, being the beer monster he was said why not, we can make it to the ground for the last half-hour. We ended up downing vodka and lime shots with the locals and staggered our way to the ground. We had only been in the ground for less than five minutes when the final whistle blew. I remember seeing little Chimmy and Ian Langford on the pitch back pedalling towards our end with around thirty lads wanting to take a piece out of them. I remember one of the lads saying come on, let's have them. How I got onto the pitch in my state I will never know.

I ended up swinging a punch and ended up on my arse hitting fresh air, the next second I was in a headlock and my arm being pushed up my back. That was the end of my contribution and in the back of the van I was in no time with a little delicate help from the Cheshire constabulary.

After being processed and seeing a few of the other lads get out from the afternoon experience I thought, it's going to be a late get out one this. Around one thirty the law throw me out of the cells, I see another figure and recognise him, it's Steve C from the moor. Another couple of lads turn up and we decide to sit in the reception area of the police station. All I can remember is being sick, the vodka had taken its toll and I was churning my stomach out. I had next to no money and kept throwing up every five minutes. Around four thirty a woman police sergeant came into the reception and threw us onto the street, she really loved me as I had made a lovely mess on her floor, her male colleagues were having a right laugh while she shoved my head in my own mess, Fuck off back to Yorkshire you mucky little twat she called me as I landed in the road, the other lads picked me up and we headed for the railway station. We had to wait for ages and ages and all the time I was in that state of gipping with nothing coming out. I borrowed the train fare and we did not get home till three in the afternoon. There are countless episodes to this meaning and another event that took place and always puts a smile on my face is the time Tats had his stag do in Bradford. Around forty of us made the trip up and you knew that this was going to be a night where it would definitely kick off. We started off in town at the Crown and made our way over to Bradford. The mood was good and we had a good crew of us. We ended up in the Old Crown, as one of the lads knew it had topless barmaids on. I have never seen so many lads surge to the bar as quick in my life to get the beers in. The girls took the stick by the lads all in good faith and no bother was to be had. The highlight of the evening in this pub was when the stripper came on and we booed her off to the delight of all the local lads, she was humiliated. She got hold of the DJ's mike and said if we could do any better than her then come and do it. Up on stage ran Knighty and Gassy. They played the same music as the stripper was dancing to and caused uproar with laughter.

The two lads had just their undies on and turned their backs to the crowd. These two had not seen each other's dicks and I think that they were having a spy on each other, Knighty not being slow realised that he was the biggest in this department and turned to the crowd swinging his hampton about, the stripper again got booed and the place was in uproar with the lads' antics. We ended up in a nightclub on the Keighley road at the top of the hill where again no trouble was had. The highlight of this was when our Willy got a bird on the dance floor and was swinging her all around, she was screaming and we found out that she had an artificial leg and got stuck on the dance floor. We left the club and headed back into town down a steep hill. We had split into two groups. Some of the lads had got something to eat and were about five hundred yards up the road. I was in the group towards the bottom end of the road when about ten very handy looking lads walked past. Both sets of lads looked at each other and they walked past, each of us weighing the other lot up. A couple of minutes past and we heard the familiar sounds. We turned and saw bodies flying all over the road. We ran back towards this lot and they did one before we got to them. All the bodies on the floor were our lot. The same thing had happened, as this lot walked past they eyed each other up and one of our lot said something, our lot were about twenty in number and fancied their chances. But these guys were like Bruce Lee, Rocky, and Ken Do Knagisaki all rolled into one, they fired in with such speed and ferocity that the lads did not know what hit them, and then they were off just as quick.

We all had a laugh walking back down and Willy shouted, where's Paul, we looked around and then back up the road, there was a body wrapped around a lamppost and we all thought it was one of them, it was Paul. When we got to him he was out cold, the law had also just arrived and we did not want to hang around, we gave them a story and we had to leave Paul there for an ambulance, his leg had been broken and he was still out, on the way home when the story was coming out it could have been some of our lads that did it as several thought at some point that he was one of them. Whatever, those lads were definitely a very handy mob. We went over to the hospital the next day and brought him home with us after he signed himself out with his pot on. No one likes leaving any of the lads but circumstances dictate this. One of the funniest I can remember is an outing to Peterborough. Peanut wanted a shit and we had parked up so the lads could get rid of the piss and have a breather. Peanut had found or so we thought a toilet box cubical at this lay-by. We all thought that he had got into this and some bright spark suggested that we roll this cubical over for the laugh, so we did. It rolled over and went down this embankment and smashed up in pieces, fuck it we thought he must be dead after that, everyone was either laughing or panicking. Peanut the sly dog was clever and had decided to have a shit round by the trees thank fuck and we all got back on the coach. Unbeknown to us, the Doctor had climbed all the way up a tree. On the coach someone shouted out was he on, this lad answered yes, but it was actually another lad by the same name, it was not till we got home that it was realised that we had left him.

Come On Then

The 80s

Chapter Fifteen
Re- Group Re-Group

We're in the old second division and we see some big name clubs and firms down at our place as well as away. I have now tended to pick and choose matches more with the responsibilities of a house and all that shit that comes with this type of life now. One team who I have not seen before is Newcastle United. Now personally speaking, I have always found the Geordie lads ok. On nights away and at races we have bumped into groups and these lads have always been friendly with no exchanges between us that I can recall. We used to have a small group of lads that always popped into Golcar if they were playing Leeds and we got on great. We even took them night clubbing on a few occasions a few years previous to this coming day. Friends or no friends though if action was called upon then we have no hesitation on what the outcome is to be. The day dawns and we meet up in the Crown in town. Everyone knows of the Geordie reputation on the black and white toon army and they must have one of the best away followings.

This rings true when we come into town; there are thousands upon thousands of the fuckers. Black and white all over and most were in big large gangs either with cider bottles and or with cans all over the joint. We start to muster a crew together and move on down the town. I can honestly say that I have never seen so bloody many boys, the nearest was when Bolton came down to my memory. All around the town skirmishes are going on, we meet a crew looking for it just up from the Wellington, a few verbal exchanges and then bang, it's off, but we are well outnumbered, we end up having to do a runner. Later on I bump into our kid. He has just been involved in one, the lads were on Cross Church street and he informs us that the lads have had to do a runner as well, big Basher went down he says, fucking loads of them, like swarming ants, we never stood a chance, once you see the big fella down he said, you new that we were for it. They went back up that year, Kevin fucking curly haired Keegan had taken over the club and great things were to come for these lads. One outstanding memory that day was after the match when a certain character from Brighouse called Paul D. he had the lads grimacing in laughter. He was stomping up and down Leeds road smacking anything in sight that was black and white demanding their scarves and whatever else he could get, fucking nuts he was and there were thousands of them, how he never got killed I do not know.

It was around this sort of time that some of our lads used to go up and watch Rangers. Its funny how the political side can come into this type of thing but at the end of the day my football team, outlook, religion and politics have always been Blue and I am also proud to be Loyal, even with a catholic sounding name. It is still the same now as it was then and when watching the England matches just look at some of the flags and see how many have the Ulster Loyalist hand symbol. I still often laugh when I recall seeing Friday in the bus station with his Orange sash around him singing "My Father wore the Sash"

We have an high population of Irish in Huddersfield and these lads were all Celtic but as I have stated before when it comes down to it, regardless of what ever, Huddersfield always stick together, the Irish lads even nicknamed our pub at the time The Crown, the "Orange Lodge"

This was truly to be the seasons of seasons with so many of the big teams about in the old second division. Again it was Leeds United down here and it had been reported in our local rag at the beginning of the season that the infamous Leeds was going to wreck our town. Now Leeds usually put on a good show and after debates on this subject we all agree that this lot have never had a result down at our place when we have played them. Yes they have put up a good show and shown resistance and at times they have come to prove a point, but again they have never had a result down here where they have walked over us.

This encounter must go down as one of the best against this lot and the volume of sheer violence that was seen that day. This was also the day that history in a sense was made with Basher and Oscar mucky bum being the first two football lads to get nicked by evidence on CCTV.

As usual all the lads were buzzing with what was to come, it always kicks off with these lads and this day was not going to be any different. Everyone met up before the match but with the police presence nothing much came about before the match. Inside the ground was different matter, running battles in the terracing took place throughout the game and a few of the boys were lifted. It was odds on there would be a major kick off outside and all the way back up Leeds road to the stadium.

It was packed that day and the congestion was unreal. The lads who numbered around sixty to seventy walked round the terracing and onto Leeds road, sure enough Leeds were there waiting and wanting the off. The lads obliged and this was one of many battles that erupted that day. It was just pure hatred violence from both sides as soon as it kicked off the old bill were about. In situations like this everyone splits up and you go with the crowd as soon as the old bill is about. The lads walked a bit trying to find each other and then the shout for the first time that day was heard, "re-group" "re-group" the lads responded to this and all came together, that was it, another bloody battle would take place, people screaming and running everywhere, it would start at one side of the road and end up at the other. Leeds seemed to be everywhere and the lads were fighting on all corners The sirens would then be off and the old bill would be there, the lads would again disperse into the crowd and the shout would go up again. What also was happening was that the Town crew was getting smaller and smaller each time the old bill fired in. They were nicking the lads like hotcakes. After the umpteenth brawl and nearing the top end of Leeds road the law were just managing to take control, some twenty five to thirty of our lads got pulled that day and although the lads were again outnumbered they kept it together and did not take a step backwards, I don't know who started the re-group shout but this event is still talked about even now and is always brought back up when reminiscing the old days.

Chapter Sixteen
The Dressers

From the early to the mid eighties, it was becoming a case of "deja-vu" A new young breed of warrior was coming through the ranks as we did in the late seventies. These lads were the dressers and affectionately known in the earlier days as the "pringleberry runners". The dressers were starting to form their own identity and lads such as Oscar, R.J. The Sheepbridge duo, and PJ were but a few to name, had come through the ranks from the early eighties with the crew.

These were to be the fore-front and elders of the yet to be formed HYC. They planned their own transport for the away matches and as the media would call it, "they were organised". They had their own residence of abode which was the Lincoln Bar where they would meet on match days. As I have stated from the Grimsby event, these lads were young and the experienced gained over the next season or two saw them developing into a formidable force in their own right.

One of the first big talking episodes that I can personally recall is when the boy's went up to the Scotland verses England match at Hamden Park. To be honest and frank, you never heard or saw the English lads up their for that sort of game and it was the same in the earlier day's when Scotland went down to Wembley, it always seemed to be full of jock's everywhere.

The new breed of youngster's were different, not just Huddersfield's lot but I suspect the same was to be said of all the youth firms up and down the country at this time. These lads wanted to impose their mark and let the other firms know just who they were. There is no better place than an England match, especially an away one, to show off your pride, muscle and strength. Even better was Scotland away.

The day dawned and the Daz Sykes organised Kenmargra coach with 50 of the top dressers departed from Huddersfield. The lads were well up for it and the mood on the coaches was electric. Everyone of those lads knew exactly what the score was, they would be greeted with a vengeance that most would not of come up against before but they knew that, they were well prepared and well up for it. A beer stop was organised at Hamilton at a boozer that one of the lads knew. At just after two the coach pulled into Hamden Park, the Scottish crowd was hostile with the usual gestures and banging on the side of the coach which seemed to be going on for ages. This was it, D-day and fuck 'em all. The lads were escorted to the ground, to say it was intimidating was an understatement, but they did not let it get to them, they sang their hearts out and let the Scottish know that they were there. They gathered with the rest of the other England lads, which numbered around another hundred or so in the terracing. They were surrounded on all corners by thousands of them. They were all screaming and baying for the Englishman's blood. What really got the lads going was the amount of flem and spit that they had to endure and that was the point when one of the dresser's thought fuck this, no more, there having some. The Huddersfield lads just streamed into them, it was like Custer's last stand, but they drove the Scot's back and really ploughed into them. This was noted by the Birmingham lads who were heard saying "stick with these Huddersfield lads, they are game as fuck". The Scots were taken back, who the fuck has the audacity to fight us on our own patch and for once they got a good taste of what we are made of. The police made the decision to move the England lads out of the ground for the reason of their own safety, but everyone else who was up there that day and especially those from our neck of the woods knows fully well that the police were shit scared of the England lads and how well they were up for it that day. Two good lads from our lot got time for that game and I do not know weather that was the start of Huddersfield's reputation within the England set up but from what I am informed it was a talking point within it.

Another personal triumph for these lads was a night game down to Cardiff in the very late eighties. The Soul Crew were making a name for themselves at this time and it had been noted as such in the usual media hype about this lot. The dresser's organised a full 50 seater and decided to pay these lads a visit and just let them know who we were.

The coach arrived in Cardiff late afternoon. As I have stated in earlier chapter's these were the times when things were getting more organised and the lads kept quite to avoid any detection. Everyone was well up for the off and on foot they marched straight to the Ninian Park Arms where it was known the "Soul Crew" would be, they arrived and marched straight into the pub, first in was RJ who had a union jack draped over his shoulder's followed by the rest of the crew. Shout's of Huddersfield filled the pub. The Taff's were a little taken back by the on surge at first and it was not long before both sides were flying into each other. The fighting spilled into the street and before it got going the law was on hand to stop it escalating. At least we did ourselves proud by turning up at their pub, which in the "Soul Crew" book, Cardiff did say that Huddersfield turned up but did not mention anything about us marching straight into their boozer for the off. At least that's another record put straight. Again backed up by the paper cut outs we had one certain well known Sheepbridge lad locked up for having his cut throat with him at that match.

That was the start of the dressers and they had many more escapades and as I have stated they had come of age and were now a force in their own right. Over the next few years some of the younger end of this lot were to start their own firm within the Huddersfield set up and become even more renowned worldwide, they would call themselves the HYC.

I would also like to take this opportunity from this chapter to single out one lad in particular. RJ from as long as I can remember and all the rest of the lads, past and present will agree with me here, that he deserves this special acknowledgement.

He was a real game lad and always in the thick of it. He has on a few occasions spent time at Her Majesty's pleasure in the cause for Huddersfield Town. On one certain occasion involving our southern friends, RJ had his liberty taken away for over two year's. A lot and I mean a lot of other people could have been in the same cell has him sharing those year's for that particular event that took place. RJ kept mum to the relief of these other people and did the time himself. A lot of you out there might not have taken the same cause or call him silly for keeping quite, but a lot of credit from lads of my era and a big thanks you echo's out to him.

RJ was and still is one of Huddersfield's Top Lads.

Chapter Seventeen
Romarnus and A New Beginning

I am Romarnus without a doubt; I am Romarnus who killed the kraut, unfortunately for those of you who are not familiar with certain characters from Huddersfield this chap is a legend in his own right.

Romarnus must go down as our best-dressed hooligan from C and A of our time if not all time. Through the late seventies and eighties this fellow always wore a jacket and trousers. He was a great advert for the man at C and A. He's a gangly six-footer plus and a game lad. Romarnus had a goal in life like many of us have only his was to meet a Leeds fan who was a Scottish copper with ginger hair, he would have killed him as well. To get to the point, his name came about when Ballbag, Airing Cupboard and he were in for the World Cup. The lads had got blotto the night before a match and a German had died, they had Romarnus on that he was the culprit because he could not remember anything.

Romarnus escapades are legend and there are too many to mention, he hated Leeds with a vengeance and on one occasion at a do, he had fallen asleep, Steve Fountain went up to him and whispered in his ear, that the dance floor was full of Leeds fans, with that Romarnus woke and darted into the middle of the dance floor kicking and punching out everywhere. He greatly exceeded himself when we got the opportunity to play Leeds away to the applause of all the lads on his one man attacking mission. As we approached the ground on the coach, he was off. His gangly frame disappearing down the road towards a tunnel next to the ground, his arms were everywhere and kung fu kicks could be seen. A few seconds later we saw him being escorted out of the tunnel between two copper horses, his feet not touching the ground.

My best recollection of this chap was when we went down to a certain nightclub at the bottom end of the Town ring road at the top of Chapel Hill. The week previous had seen one of our boys whose dad used to play for Huddersfield once upon a time get a bit of a slapping for trying to help a lad who was greatly outnumbered. We thought we would take a look and just see what this group were like when it came to even numbers. The omens were there that night as on the way down the Grouch ended up having a right old beano one on one with a well known hard man. It was one of those five minutes of pure fighting across from the Co-op on the precinct. Such was the ferocity of the fight and neither one giving an inch we pulled them apart and they called it a do. That set the stall and you knew one way or another it would kick off for sure. We all got into the club and the beer was as usual going down well. There were a few different types in, skins, punks, student types and the usual beer monsters. It was looking a no go, as this gang we were looking for had not turned up. I remember being down by the cloakroom and heard that familiar sound of breaking glass, I looked over and saw the lads, it was off. The bouncers and some of their mates had been arguing with a few of the lads and that was it, no questions asked it was straight in and at them. I remember seeing Romarnus and his arms flying around, the checked jacket gave it away. The best shot of the night came when our local tattooist who was with these blokes got involved and was just taking his jacket off, he had it half way round his arms and I planted him with the perfect punch, the Gouch could not stop laughing at that one. As usual with this type of thing, it spilled out into the street. The sirens could be heard and we started making our way back up to town. The bouncers' mates were following us, I can remember seeing three of these lads approaching, the were tying their belts around their fists, all of a sudden a fucking dustbin was hurtling through the air towards these three who quickly moved out of the way. It swayed and slowed them down. I turned and saw Romarnus grinning and dusting his hands off, fucking rubbish he grins then turns around looking for something else to throw. He is a good lad and still gets down to the matches and is a character in his own right.

It's coming up to the end of the eighties and what a good year it's been. I have just ended my marriage after a very short period and feel good. I think it was always on the cards, I do not think that I met with her family's expectations, but no disrespect to any one at all, that's life and I came away for the better of it all. I move in with my mate Max and start to enjoy the single life. The rave scene is here and has been in a while and one of my Golcar mates Blyth as been at the front of it for a while now. I have always been one for a good time and loved a dance and this new wave that everyone seems to be enjoying is just what I was looking for. I also had plenty of money in my pocket and started visiting the casino and was living the high life. Tracey my lovely wife has always stated that one of my problems has always been that I always throw myself in deeply and addict myself to things.

I can't just have a flutter or a one off I have to go the whole hog and that is what I did. The rave scene as many of you can associate with came with the drugs and yes, I also got involved with them as did everyone else.

This went on a while and it got to the stage where my old mate Max had to have a good word with me along with a clip round the ear. Thank heaven for the mates that I have and I listened to what he said and took the advice. It was a good while it lasted and I was again back on the straight and narrow. After a while I met the girl of my dreams, totally different from my previous wife and I was hooked straight away. Now ask any good man and he will agree with this next sentence. Behind every good man there is an even better woman. We courted and she gave me the honour of becoming my wife and soul mate. She is the best thing ever in my life and how she has moulded me and made me a better person, she has stood by me where other women would not with their men, I was a bugger in the beginning of our relationship and she must have seen something in me, she's the best and any advice I could give to any lad is that you will always have a good life with a good woman with you. I love her to bits and she bore me two beautiful girls, to which I owe her my life for that. That made our family complete with Tracey's two sons from her previous marriage, David and Matthew.

Gradually, those fun filled days disappeared with the football, with the exception of a Christmas special or a big cup game and that part of my life was now in the past and I had settled down to married life, I had progressed in my work and we then eventually moved to our own house.

As life travelled on and the kids grew, money was ok and I was now nearing my mid to late thirties, Tracey said why don't you go down to the matches every now and then. It was around this time when if we went up the village, the stories were coming back on new adventures with the now older crew.

Some never left and others had started drifting back, Town were doing well and we had gone up to the first division, a new ground and a healthier looking mob of older lads, the new generation of HYC which was being headed by one of the top lads who was called Chinks, things were more organised and the stories were great.

Of our old mob, and still going was Syko, The Silver Fox Knighty, Nige, Phil, Bob, Mr C of Brighouse, Rick, Max, Goffer and a few others, there were still some of the old mobs whose numbers had now dwindled and we used to get together for at least several away days. That was it, I was again hooked and started to go back down with the boys.

AJM was still and is still active and organised a reunion to Millwall, a fantastic day out but no bother, the other thing I noticed was how well the law had organised itself as well. The younger lot gave us the name of the OAPs which later progressed to the over forty's these lads were still up for it if it was to happen and it surely did do,

We mainly loved the away days because we used to call off for a beer and enjoy ourselves, we were different from the official hooligans and older, but in the enemy's eyes, we were still a target.

Tracey as usual gave me her blessing and said get off, organised by the Silver Fox that weekend was an away day to Blackburn.

Chapter Eighteen

The Silver Fox, Here
We Go Again

There was a racing trip and most of the OAP from our crew had gone on it, an expensive boot and suit racing job which they had been saving for over the year, so it was left with three of us on the early morning train, we had heard on the grapevine that the HYC was going over in force with this lot dropping down from the premiership and showing them how it was done. We arrive in Blackburn and have a good day on the beer and trounced the bookies, we don't actually see the young ones but in several pubs we hear that they have arrived and can tell that they have met with the Blackburn crew, sirens were wailing every now and then. We get to the ground and to top it all we end up losing the match. We then decide to walk back into town for a few bevvies before the crowd. We're just on the outskirts on a dual carriage and can see a mob of around fifteen Town youth about five hundred yards ahead, we then notice a group of around forty Blackburn over the other side of the carriageway, the Fox gives me the nod, we've got company, they fly over the carriageway wanting their vastly outnumbered opponents. The young ones stand but a few then bolt down the road, they manage to get hold of one of the HYC lads and around five of them are giving him a kicking, now this is not on, fair enough when the odds are even, but when you outnumber the opposition like that a slap and a crack is ok, but one lad on his own, the Fox shouts, "any law Tel Boy", I look around and can see another small mob of Blackburn at the back of us, panicking and losing the old bottle a bit I shout over to Fozzer NO, leave it, he thinks I mean no law and streams straight in at these lot, me and the other lad have no option but to follow through with him, the Fox is having a field day, he's loving every minute, the next thing I know is that some twat is flinging me around by my hood and I fall in front of a bus on the carriageway, the other lot from behind have collared me, we hold our own as these Blackburn youth are a little bewildered at the sight of these old ones streaming in at them, it settles down with a bit of mouthing.

One of their big ones is giving it a bit and we have managed to get the young Huddersfield lad free, the Fox asks this geezer for the lad's hat back, the Fox then head butts the big one and downs him in one, these lot are now really pissed off, we are greatly outnumbered and it's time to back off and we start to leg it back up the road, the Fox, god bless, still wants to fight all of them. What would most people have done in that situation, I must admit, I shit myself, my heart was pounding, it had been seven or eight years since I had been involved in anything like that, it was same with the other lad, but the Fox is one on his own, no fear, it comes about that the lad taking the kicking was from Golcar, we saw some of the lads he had been with later in the station and gave them a bollocking, it's the same old story, stick together, Oscar mucky bum was at the station and laughing at us with the young casual squad, Oscar has been around for a few years and never looks any older, he started his trade with us lot and can still give it large when needed. The Fox just laughed it off, he loves it, he's taking the piss in the pub and says we should not have legged it, he is right though, but at our age and having around forty Blackburn wanting to tear the living life out of you takes a bit of getting back in to.

Knighty and the other lads all laugh when they get to know about it all and Mr I know it all (Knighty) then tells us what would have happened if he and the usual crew had been there and not the two apprentices the Fox had to put up with.

We have turned into a new millennium and again it's picking and choosing the matches. I have just started a new job with a brilliant firm with whom I am still working. It's not a bad crack with the Leeds lads that work there and we have a few bets and take the piss. The money is even better and that means a few more days out with the boys. Our next jaunt away is Rotherham, we go by train and we have around twenty five of us, from the OAP squad, the Fox had seen to a boozer over here and wanted to call in, no bother before the match although we get the eye a few times in the town centre and just before the ground. We decide to pop into town again after the match, we are told when we enter this pub that this is the Rotherham boys' pub, again no turn up, we stayed for two beers and then moved on, we have with us on a first a lad called Webbo, he is over six foot odd and an ex rugby player, he is a quite lad and very very handy, step brother to the infamous Jimmy Johnson, who I mentioned earlier, we also have another lad on his first with us but who has been around over the years and he's also a very very handy lad, Yatesy. We visit a few pubs and end up on the main street in the centre. I can't remember the name of this one but it was at the top end of the main road and there are quite a few lads in and Rotherham youth, they probably have a few more in numbers but they're mostly at the youth to thirties age. We sit in a room, the cards are out and we are enjoying ourselves but also keeping an eye on the situation, it's going to go off in here, the lads have all sat behind us and they are all supping bottles, silly twats, as though we are going to fall for that, again the Fox nods and whispers a few words around this other table and also to two other lads that have come into the pub, these are beer monsters and not fighters, the Fox warns them, another few come in and behind us they are smoking weed, Knighty asks one of these lads for some and the reply was what we expected, anyway, Nige and Goffer are sick of waiting and decide to start it for them, one of these lads grabs his bottle, before he can raise it I have hit him over the head with a buffet, it's off, we pound into them with speed and ferocity, more have joined their ranks and they try to put up a bit of a do. I remember seeing the big lad, Webbo being the last out with at least six of them trying to get hold of him, he is playing it with ease and has not even reached second gear. It spills into the street and we fan out across the road, they come onto us, we don't back off, it's good hand to hand and they start to put on a bit of a show, down this main street more lads are coming out of the pubs, Yatesy, a fearsome looking bugger shouts at one group to fucking get back in and keep out of it, these lot are now trying to get round our flanks, the law is here and it's little pockets of fighting here and there, I look over and Nige and Goffer charge at a group of six or seven, Nige goes down, I run over and jump into the middle of the group, they have no balls especially as the law are in amongst us, the Fox lets rip into one of the mouthy fuckers and he gets nicked, we are marched off by the law, these lads disperse. We call for one last one before the last train out of this place, we expect a comeback, and again no show and the law are shadowing us. The Silver Fox has struck again, he has a very nice little business and at his age should not be getting arrested, but as he says, it never goes away when it comes on and he certainly will not leave his mates in the shit. He has a wicked smile and all the time I have known him he has been a good man, he always takes time out and if anyone has any bother you no he will be there without asking.

Chapter Nineteen
The OAPs

This was the name bestowed to our little group from Oscar and the younger HYC boys.

Our main abode of residence was the Bradley Mills School club just off the Leeds road and the main walkway to the new stadium. It's a lovely club and ninety percent of the clientele on a Saturday was the older lads have ourselves with the other crews who were ageing into the later thirties along with the lads who were just reaching the forties. We were well known and even at this age we were a match for anyone who thought otherwise as big Bruce once put it, we're getting on a bit, but we can still do the business when required.

We have had some big name lads and crews come in and they have all showed us the respect we command, firms from Sunderland, Birmingham and Middlesborough are a few to mention. There have been a few skirmishes outside like the time the Silver Fox and Goffer staged a two-man assault on a mini bus of Birmingham lads after they had been giving it the come on. On that particular occasion they both charged to confront the occupants of this bus who were jumping off to trade their business and the Fox was confronted by a midget who was one of the first off! Sirens were sounding and cars wailing around to the amusement of the HYC who had not been able to meet their counterparts on an arranged fight, they were heard as saying, "fucking OAPs are at it the lucky bastards" as they stood waiting at the top of Leeds road and never had a sniff that day due to the police presence. Away days were our forte and as time went on the group got bigger and we became a tidy mob.

One of the best home scraps for the OAPs has to be when Barnsley came down, I have mentioned previously and after this event that these lads are no mugs and again credit where it is due. The lads had been on the town and called in the school just before the match for the last couple of beers, the usual crowd were in and a few shirts from Barnsley and the older end were in and the mood was as good as it gets on these derby matches.

Knighty and Phil decided not to bother with the match as the rest of the lads went to the ground. The beer taste was in and they decided a few more beers and a game of cards was a better offer.

A while later the two were playing against each other when they noticed a big group of lads our own age group descend upon the club. Knighty knew instantly that this lot was Barnsley before they had opened their mouths. These lads then noticed that Knighty and Phil were playing cards and asked to join in. All went well for a while and Knighty could do no wrong and was taking the money in left right and centre. One of the Barnsley lads then accused Knighty of cheating because he was winning everything. Knighty laughed and told him he would be an idiot with all them around to try that, the other Barnsley lads were ok and calmed this geezer down. The game was then finished and it was then not long before the other lads started to drift in as the match was now over. One of the first of our lot in was the Silver Fox and Syko, as they walked in they had noticed that this lot were Barnsley. A few of the other OAP's then began drifting in and, the Fox flew in and a wild west type brawl was off in seconds. Ricky had his lad with him who he stood in one corner and said, stay there and don't let your Mother know what I have been up to and with this, proceeded to thump anything that moved that was not from Huddersfield. Syko, one of our big guns had been held back by a bloke of around sixteen stone who fell on him and he could not move. The Fox had hold of one of these lads in a head lock and was telling Peanut to thump him, when he did, the Fox shouted at him to thump him and not tap him.

All around the old fellas were joining in and the Barnsley lads started backing off towards the doorway entrance although they did give a good account of their self's. The law was soon about and both sets of lads abided by the code and no arrests were made. The usual laughter was abundant once the dust settled and the piss taking was being dished out. A young lad of around seventeen was moaning to his dad who had been piling in about having a sore jaw. The Dad answered back and told him to shut up and stop moaning. What do you expect lad he says, you take a gamble on firing in, you expect to be belted back, make sure you do better next time. I did hear a time after that these same lads went back on another visit and belted a few lads, none of the originals were in though, maybe next time lads eh. As time went on I was drifting back in and out of the game, but always managed to make a turn out for the big ones. We later then called ourselves the over forty club. The buzz was still there and at times it was like going back in time, really looking forward to the away days and getting all excited. My own personal view was that the camaraderie was even stronger than before, perhaps with age and a smaller crew this shone through on respect and knowing who exactly was where if an event did break out. I even remember Doug making calling cards, which were inscribed with the usual stuff, Welcome you've just met the Huddersfield's over forty boys.

We have had our fun on the away days, which I have mentioned in other chapters and the big one was Wolves. We then had a reunion to Millwall away organised by AJM and myself, which was a real turn out of the old boys. We stayed at one of the Brighouse lads' brother's pub in London and a great day out was had by all. Our next reunion is Port Vale away and with writing this book and seeing the old lads again it's all buzzing like mad, both AJM and myself are again the organisers and we were booked up in the first couple of days. It just shows that as time goes past and we all move on it's still in the blood and it's all of us who think the same. My phone has never stopped and between you and me the same conversation keeps cropping up, wonder if it will kick off. Most are turning round and saying we're too old for this, but it's at the back of everyone's mind and fuck it, if it does, we can hold our own. Who knows, I may have another chapter yet on the outcome of this?

Chapter Twenty

The HYC and The
Scottish Connection

Most club firms have names, Huddersfield just before
the turn of the nineties became known as the HYC. I
knew some of the lads associated with them when I came
back into the fold. The residence of abode, is a pub called
the Crescent and they have on a full turn out around
two hundred to two hundred and fifty upwards, they
are very well organised and from what I am informed
well respected in the England set up. I went down to the
Bradford match and had seen how times had changed.
The pub was packed to the beams and had a mixture of
young and old. A shout came up and the entire pub went
quiet, Bradford had rung to say that they were just up the
road at the Slubbers Arms and would be down shortly for
the off.

Sure enough within ten minutes the shout from a
couple of scouts came through that they were here. A mob
of around one hundred turned up and I have never seen

a pub empty so quickly, even when I have been singing Mac the Knife on the Karaoke. The foray began swiftly with the HYC giving their counterparts a quick turnover. It lasted all of two minutes but good on Bradford and top marks for showing up even though they knew they would be outnumbered. They got escorted away after the match but returned later that night into town for another go.

When I started going down again to the new stadium, I noticed a flag with the words St Johnson and HTFC, I had no idea at the time of who these lads were but it later transpired that up to twenty and more at a time would come down to the matches and were fully fledged lads associated with the HYC.

Bonds and ties had been made in Spain on a working holiday and the Scottish lads invited down to Huddersfield.

The new breed and generation were a different lot and it was nice to see that we still had a good firm, I was hearing some good stories about this lot.

They take no prisoners and at a cup game against Derby I knew the reason as to why. We are on the top tier at the John Smiths stand, underneath are all the HYC boys. What started it I do not know but when the law intervened on something in the middle of this lot, all hell broke loose, and severe toe to toe slugging, baton welding action was taking place, law or no law, when someone goes over the top, lads will not tolerate this and that is what happened. This went on for quite a while and the lads eventually drove the police back to the edge of the pitch. Order was then restored with a massive amount of police and stewards. One of the lads turned round and said that was worth the entrance fee alone watching that.

On the Monday night in the Examiner the local paper, there was a rogues gallery and we all had a chuckle as the Doctor was one of them, they all got time for that along with banning orders.

One of the top boys in the HYC was Chinks, he was well respected by all and also very well known in the England set up.

Things were more organised in this day and age and the mobile phone was a very good source of communication and arranging battles out of the way and avoiding detection and arrests.

Most firms would meet on the England games and arrange such sorties and swap telephone numbers. One of the top firms around and who where making a name for themselves at this time were Stoke City.

Over the years I cannot really say that we ourselves have come across them, but respect where it's due.

It was inevitable that as it does, the HYC would come across these lads and they did. England were playing Ireland away, around forty of the HYC got on the train for the game, most had walked through the carriage which was full of England lads throughout the train, Chinks, Inchy and another lad were the last three on and some lads started taking the piss over one of these lads calling him Bob Marley and asking him for a reefer, who are you lot Chinks asked, Stoke was the reply, Inchy said, I will give you a fucking reefer and poked this geezer in the eye with his finger, that started it, Chinks piled in and in the melee got his foot stuck on the seating and took a beating, the other boys noticed what was going on and fired in, but with only so much space and other lads trying to stop it, this cooled off a bit. At Holyhead the lads were really angry, Stoke or no fucking Stoke, this was getting sorted, as soon as they got off the train they piled into this lot, a bloody battle took place in which the HYC were giving it Stoke well and it ended up with other mobs joining the Stoke ranks. The Law to avert any more trouble would not let the HYC onto the ferry and sent them back.

To give Stoke their respect, they came up to Huddersfield on the day of a match at ten in the morning to the Dog and Gun, then the HYC residence of abode, Chinks, Oscar and another half dozen of the HYC were in the top end pool room and saw the mass ranks of this mob and did one before they got to them. Once the lads mobbed up endless running battles took place throughout the day, this lot never bothered with the match and it was obvious they had come up to make a point of it. Respect or not, when you are on home ground you have to hold it and although heavily outnumbered on that day, the re-grouped HYC stood and fought in the face of adversity and can keep their heads held high on this particular event.

Chinks recalls another time was when England were playing Sweden, after some sorties before the match as usual the law enforcement was in no mood and had dished a bit of stick out to the England boys. Inside the ground, Chinks had got one of the Swedish flags and torched it, all the lads were cheering and spitting on it, the ultimate insult. The police were obviously getting really wound up and a voice from the back of Chinks called out, you lot, we will back you up if the law start. Who are you lot Chinks asks, Stoke was the reply, fuck you lot and with that, the lads laid into them. Another firm that seemed to crop up for the odd battle at the England matches against the HYC was Villa. On one particular encounter Villa were chasing some of the lads onto the train, one in particular was Robbo, Chinks jumps up at the doorway and tells these Villa to fuck off. Listen mate they say, we just want the nigger, fuck you says Chinks, you are not having the nigger, at this point Robbo pops up from behind and starts having a go at Chinks and tells him not to call him a nigger, bewildered at the argument between them the Villa left, this is what camaraderie is all about. The HYC have mixed it well with the firms from this era and were well known. There have been countless battles with our Yorkshire neighbours and one well-documented episode was when Barnsley came into town one weekend night on a stag do. All the Barnsley lads were dressed up in seventies gear and had been around the town for a while. Word had got around a crew was assembled which was mostly the HYC lads. A raging battle took place and myself and Max were on the town that night when it actually happened, the police had cordoned off Cross Church street where the bloody toe to toe battle was taking place. To give Barnsley their due, in the book they stated that Huddersfield where well outnumbered but put up such a ferocious fight. It's not often the other side will tell it as it is and that is why I have myself put these boys with our episodes in the frame for what they are.

Our other so-called neighbours of Leeds also came into town one night on a stag do. Again these lads knew where they were going and headed straight into the Crescent. Chinks was in and knew that this lot were out of towners. Some of the other HYC boys were playing pool round the corner and at first were not aware as to what was about to happen. This Leeds lot proceeded to cause mayhem and when one of the lads went flying past the poolroom the lads then set about them. Credit where it's due and this lot put up a good show and respect for turning up at the Crescent where they knew they would get one.

An Apology

On the first printing, a story involving a certain person from London was published. This story involving stoke was not correct and the person named should not have been. No harm or embarrassment on anyone's behalf was intent and I do apologies for this.

Chapter twenty-one
HYC
The Battle of Turin

I have never had the opportunity of being at an England match abroad. I have always wanted to but for some reason or another I have never managed it. The nearest is when I went to Marseille when Manchester United was there in the European Cup and I went with a red from work, but that's another story.

In the early days it was Daz Sykes who organised a coach for the England matches at home and I have had the pleasure several times watching them at home. The forerunners as I call them on the away matches aboard that I can first recall were Ball Bag, Romarnus and Airing Cupboard who went in the early eighties. These lads were part of our set up but money was a big problem in the early days and these lads with their jobs had this and the time. From our inner crew in the late eighties and early nineties it was Fountain who set the precedent and he was involved several times with the violence that attributed the game in them days. They even got a mention in a book written by an Arsenal fan. As I have stated it was Chinks' lot who really put Huddersfield on the map and gained the respect within the hooligan fraternity.

No more so was this, than in the World Cup of nineteen ninety. The lads had been there in Italy for most of the matches and had had the usual playtime with the locals, police and other mobs within the set up.

The mood in the camps had been irritable by the presence of the local constabulary and the usual media hype on the hooligan element, which at times has played more than a part in setting up bother one way or another to grab the headlines and put another nail in our coffins.

The lads had travelled up from Naples after the qualifying group and the atmosphere was good amongst the England lads, Huddersfield had a good turn out and they were positioned at the end of this camp in Turin. Word was spreading around the camp that the Italians were going to pay the camp a visit on a revenge mission for the lives that were lost in Belgium against Liverpool. No one on the first night gave a fuck and the attitude especially from the Huddersfield boys was let them come. The numbers from the Huddersfield entourage were growing steadily with the mouthwatering event to come with the Germans and a lot of the older end were by this time turning up, the mood was good and everyone was enjoying themselves. The next day arrived and the Argentinians knocked out the Italians, the lads had an idea on what might happen next, they were right. The riot police turned up in force and started to surround the camp. The HYC then took matters into their own hands and started to get tooled up with everything they could get their hands on. DT arrived out of nowhere with a tractor and unit. The unit went over for a barricade and the petrol pipes on the tractor were cut and petrol bombs were then made for the off. A mob of Italians made an appearance but as usual in their history of fighting they did not last, especially when the first of the petrol bombs flew over to them. The police retaliated with smoke bombs and that was just the starter for the night. Running battles erupted with the lads retreating and then the riot police in turn retreating. Huddersfield were the brunt that kept the England lads at it, after several hours with a smoke filled camp and tiredness setting in, the numbers started to dwindle, light came and the police themselves were heading back home to leave four scarfed lads still throwing slates and whatever else they could at them. The four jumped in ecstasy at the departing enforcement. Chinks turned round and knew that one of the other lads was DT, he turned to the other two lads and asked who they were. One was from Holland and the other was of an oriental cast, what the fuck you doing he asks, well these other two said, we knew it would kick off here and we wanted a bit, well they sure did and when it was highlighted on TV at home it was big Watty who was on the cameras.

That was not the last of it, this was the day we played the Germans in the semi finals. More Huddersfield was by now joining the ranks for this game and the HYC and all had tickets for the German end. The lads managed to get into the ground and we all to this day know what happened. The fuckers beat us on penalties and I will never forget that smarmy German bastard's stance when he scored the winning penalty, the cameras never showed it but the HYC after the game gave them hell. Strategically positioned with being in with them they took it to the core of the German lads and gave it to them good style.

France 92 was another blinder in which the HYC were at the forefront of all the action and again their reputation and respect was growing all the time. As you will see from the newspaper report cut outs, we were always in the thick of it and have never shied away from anything. Again the photos will back up the stories you see and again it was the HYC who again dealt it out against Poland over there.

Sweden away was another battle in which Chinks had a broken leg. Chinks ended up in the cells and found himself in the company of the self-proclaimed top hooligan of that time Paul Dodds. The law had been giving the lads a bit of a hard time so they decided to dish some back. When the cell door opened up a couple of the lads who had borrowed Chink's crutches laid into them, and drove them back. That did the trick and the law gave them some respect for that little excursion. So Mr Dodds, you get a mention in our book but did not live up to your promise to mention Chinks in yours.

HYC Italy 90

Chinks & Daz with the HYC

Sheepbridge Loyal

Robbo and the lads just kicking off in Poland

The famous 4, Turin aftermath

Oscar, PJ and Daz and some of the other lads in France

Football supporters accused of blackening name of Huddersfield

FIGHTING FANS
IN FERRY BAN

By ANDREW HIRST

THIRTY-FIVE soccer fans from Huddersfield were barred from getting on a ferry after brawling broke out at a Welsh port.

The hooligans had been trying to get over to Ireland for today's soccer international against England when fighting broke out on the train station concourse at Holyhead just before 2am.

Police broke up the skirmishes and the 35 fans were put on a train and sent out of the town.

British Transport police stayed on the train until it reached Chester to make sure the fans caused no more trouble.

Mr Brian Rees, a spokesman for ferry firm Stena Sealink, said the fans had been due to board the Stena Hibernia roll-on roll-off ferry for the 2.40am sailing.

But he added: "There was no way we were taking idiots like that on our ship, so we turned them away.

"We are just not prepared

shame on their town if they misbehave.

"The name of Huddersfield is blackened this morning."

Anglesey police commander Supt Alun Jones said security at the port was tight and the troublesome fans were dealt with quickly.

He revealed that the fans from Huddersfield had clashed with supporters from the Stoke area — but the Stoke fans were allowed on board the ferry.

"I don't know why they were let on," he said. "That decision was taken by officers dealing with the incident and the ferry company."

Mr Rees added: "Anyone who got on board that ferry must not have been considered a threat to other passengers.

Supt Jones said: "The fans from Huddersfield were not allowed on because of fears for the safety of other passengers.

"It was a night sailing in bad weather and the last thing the ferry staff needed was trouble in the confined

Local fans in capital
during after-game riot

By CHRIS MELLOR

HARDLINE soccer fans from Huddersfield were in London at the time of the Wednesday night riot in Trafalgar Square, say police.

There had been reports that some of them were involved in the trouble, but today the Metropolitan Police incident room, investigating the violence, could not confirm this.

Soccer hooligans ran riot in the London square following England's penalty shoot-out defeat by Germany at Wembley.

Pc Dave Hobart, of the

Metropolitan Police incident room, said fans from Huddersfield had been stopped at the Metropolitan Police boundary in North London earlier in the day.

He said fans in a number of mini-buses had been stopped to see if they had any weapons, if they had tickets and to find out what they were doing in London.

He said the Huddersfield fans were in London without tickets and were not at the match.

Soccer hooligans have also been blamed for damaging shop windows in Huddersfield on Wednesday.

HYC altercation with Stokes N40

itched battle as rivals clash before

SOCCER FAN
WRECK PUB

By Simon Penfold and Mark Cotton

Picture: P18

RE THAN 150 rival football fans involved in a pitched battle out- a Wolverhampton pub this after-, leaving the premises wrecked.

Four Huddersfield men flown home from Sweden

Disgraced Town fans deported

By NEIL ATKINSON

DISGRACED Huddersfield Town fans in Sweden for the European Championships have been deported.

The four Huddersfield men were in a group of 10 who were flown into Luton last night on a special charter jet, accompanied by Swedish police officers, after nights of violence.

The four Huddersfield men are in their 20s and early 30s and are said to be regulars at Huddersfield Town matches, both home and away.

Police confirmed that the 10 fans had been rounded up on a train travelling from Malmo to Stockholm — scene of tonight's vital Championship match between England and the host nation.

England had played their first two games in Malmo and the city was the scene of several nights of rioting and violence.

The fans were allegedly travelling on the train without tickets but police have confirmed they were also questioned about alleged thefts.

After a night in police cells in Stockholm, the fans were put on a small jet for the two-hour flight to Luton.

One of the Huddersfield fans arrived home and told reporters that other fans had been causing the trouble. "I may have tattoos but that does not make me a hooligan. The police had no idea how to control the situation and the trouble was not caused solely by English fans."

The deportations are the first by the Swedish authorities, who have arrested 122 Englishmen in the eight days of the Championships.

Police in Sweden are hoping that their softly-softly tactics will prevent trouble at tonight's vital game, but tension is mounting in the Swedish capital.

Stockholm was relatively peaceful overnight despite the presence of 2,000 English fans and groups of rival Swedes. Police are maintaining a large but low-key presence on the streets.

The England supporters have been barred from giant tents selling cheap beer after the violence in Malmo, which had centred on similar tents.

Details of the fans who have been deported or arrested have been passed to British Police and to the football authorities.

Mr George Calligan, Huddersfield Town's safety officer, said: "If these people have been involved with any disorder, we as a club will co-operate with any action that the authorities want us to take.

"We do not want anything to do with football hooligans at Huddersfield Town."

Asst Chief Constable Malcolm George, who is in Stockholm to liaise with Swedish police, warned that further violence could see England becoming the soccer outcasts of Europe.

HYC deported from Sweden

Chapter Twenty-two
The Big One

Each and every one of us at some time is involved in that special one. The big one that we all remember and it's usually a great victory against all the odds. There have been many occasions where events have taken place that could fit into this category for what ever reason and I have been involved in several heart stopping situations like these but this story for me along with most of the lads has to be the big one. Looking back over time and the years I can honestly say that this will stay with me forever, and again after talking with most other lads from that day, they also agree with me that this was definitely the best. It was our involvement with Wolves when we played them away. This one to me is the big one for several reasons, the whole day was brilliant, you could not have planned it any better and the outcome is what heroes are made of .The camaraderie that was involved from the beginning of the morning through the whole day, the way we all stuck together and the result of it all at the end.

It was to be one of my last trips away for a long time, it was Wolves away. Syko had organised to drive us in a small bus and we all agreed on a breakfast at the Rose and Crown from Golcar. The mood and laughter was in great form with a good top crew of the over forties gathered.

The beer was going down well and the rib taking was fast flowing with Knighty leading the front of it all. Bullit kept asking me if us Golcar lot knew how to brush our teeth with the bad smell of breath and to make matters better I was paired to be sat next to the twat on the coach. The talk on the day was of old days and what we used to get up to and whether we would come up against anything was flowing.

We all know that Wolves are a big, big club and have got a good crew behind them. The journey did not seem to take that long and of course the talk then came up about the HYC and the Wolves firm. We had heard on the grapevine that a meeting between the two firms had been organised and the showdown event was to be just on the outskirts of Wolves at a place called Ironbridge.

We feel we have taken the quieter option with agreeing to go into the city and not encounter a big one with the meeting already taking place elsewhere. It's not the bother we are worried about but the thought of getting nicked at our age with most of us married with kids and good jobs.

We arrive in Wolves around eleven thirty and park up, we are cautious and are moved away from one pub just outside the ground. We end up just around the corner at a gaff called the Shakespeare. Now this is a very big pub and it seemed quiet enough and the landlady had no problem with the opposing fans coming in and having a beer. It seemed friendly enough and the locals that were in at this time were also ok. Meanwhile, over at the pre-arranged meeting at the grapevine, the two coach loads of the HYC had turned up at the planned venue. They go towards the pub that the meeting was aimed for. They see lads in bushes and windows making signals like boxes and so forth, what the fuck are they doing Chinks says, one of the lads replies, playing fucking charades, let's fuck them. What the Wolves lads were trying to tell them was that the law was about with cameras and videos and that they were waiting for them. This venture had been well organised and planned on both sides, with only a handful of the top boys knowing the exact location of the planned meet, no mobiles or communication was planned right up to the last minute and the HYC was not expecting any old bill about. The HYC stormed the pub smashing it to bits and some of the lads even managed to get in the back way and extract some action against them. The whole episode was filmed and documented and court cases were brought. It transpires that the HYC had a mole informing the police, this person was then identified through a process of elimination. Back in Wolves we are still at the same place and stay all day, the landlord is ok with us and the fans that are in are mostly shirts and a few our age group. The pub steadily fills up and we keep our guard and do not let our eye off the ball. Again the beer is flowing and the cards are in full swing. The Fox and Syko decide to pop up to the other boozer for a recci and make sure that the bus is ok. We are mostly situated at the far end of the pub playing cards and a few of the boys are playing pool, again up to now, the locals have been ok and we have not sensed any problems on the horizon. Rick is playing pool with a local and it's been noticed that a few lads have come in and are sizing us up. Another small group appear and the lad who is playing pool with Rick says, here mate, you better get back with your mates, this lot here will tear your arms and legs off, they're really bad, now we have seen what's coming and have not made any move. I pop into the toilet and Nige is in, hurry up he says, fuck this lot, let's give it them before they start. We later find out that the crew that has just turned up is part of there main firm, or should I say what's left of them.

As stated the HYC had turned out in force at the pre-arranged meeting and had done the business against them good time. What transpired was that these lads are a little upset and have been licking their wounds and have obviously heard that some Huddersfield is in the Shakespeare.

I sit back down on the card table and someone says, don't go to the bar, these lot are going to start, Bullit had gone over to the pool table to get Rick. Mr C and big Brighouse Nige are also over there, at this point as Bullit is walking over and a geezer asks where he is from, Bullit replied, "Huddersfield" the fucker then nuts him, that's it we're off.

The main lot of them charge at us, we were ready and knew what was to come. The table was up and we are at them, glasses and bottles were smashing all over and that familiar noise of shouting when these circumstances arise. The trouble we now have here is that our group is split into two and we are making sure we head towards the smaller group who are at it like hammer and tong.

I just see Mr C take down two of them with a cue, we force them back and re-group and head towards the door, all the time one on ones and little group skirmishes are going on, bottles and glasses and stools are flying all over, the shirts and other locals are getting caught up in the middle and total panic and mayhem with all the screaming is going on, We then manage to get through a side door. I notice once outside that there must be one hundred and thirty to one hundred and fifty shirts and other fans that had now turned their attention to the noise and commotion that was occurring outside. Leading their lot is a mouthy blond haired lad with a silly teeshirt on, he's shouting get the black bastard, in reference to Webbo, Webbo is the last out and manages to get this mouthy twat in the doorway. Webbo along with a few more are giving him a good belting and shouting who's the black bastard now then eh! We spill onto the road and automatically fan the width of it! All their firm are now outside and it's raining bottles and glasses everywhere, they are helped with some of the shirts and locals, they must number around two hundred outside the pub, we have seventeen and two of our finest in Syko and the Fox are in another boozer. Golcar Nige gets belted with a bottle on the head, a lot of blood, he's out of it, we form a tight line and they charge us, webbo shouts don't move, if anyone moves I will sort them later, We are still armed with chairs and glasses, they stop, what the fuck is going on, they outnumber us at least four or five to one. Mr C always one to spot a weakness shouts, come on, they haven't got it, let's fucking charge them, we move up to them and a few exchanges take place. Peanut flies into them with a broken chair leg, I pick up a broken glass and throw it at one who receives it full in the face, he's down, one of the lads finishes him off with a good boot,

I run round our line to the other end where big Nige is trying to take on four of them, a couple of us fly in, we are backing off a bit but still when they have the numbers I cannot understand how they have not overpowered us, they just keep edging and mouthing, all this time we are holding our ground and are a little bemused, we are all surprised but what we learn later was that it was a tactical move by their firm. The fuckers, they wanted to keep us on the back road away from the main street just around the corner, so that another mob of around forty which had gone round the top end of the pub, and then all the way around to trap us. As they charged round the bottom of the road they were confronted by the law, which at that point had just turned up behind our lines. It was nice in a sense to hear the sirens and we knew then that we had done it and what made it all the sweeter was that Wolves main firm had had it twice that day, once from the Huddersfield main firm of the HYC in Ironbridge which gave them a good belting and again by the vastly outnumbered OAPs

The Town coaches are passing us at this point on the main road as we are heading towards the ground, you can see the looks on some of the faces as though to say, look at that lot, you'd think at their age they would learn, but fuck it, it was a great result and the Silver Fox was gutted. We had no opposition after the match either, funny they knew where we were parked, the young HYC after learning of our events laughed all day.

2000

Chapter Twenty-three
HYS
Tact and Tactics

Only this week did I hear a story that actually moved me and kept my faith in the human race. It is not very often that you hear of stories about men of violence who succumb to the sorrow that held a nation and who shared in the sorrow that this tragedy caused. I was introduced to another young man who is well known throughout the HYC of this present time whilst having a quick drink with my old mate Syko in the Rose and Crown up Golcar.

Carlton is a big lad and well renowned with everyone and we all got chatting about the book, he as others have been was at first sceptical over my inquiries to the youth of today. They now called themselves the HYS, Huddersfield youth squad. Once a little bit of trust was gained certain stories come over which I thought would be very good material to put into print. Then Carlton proceeded to tell me the story of the day Town were playing Peterborough away. Suddenly his mood had changed to that of triumphant on the previous stories and both Syko and myself listen with intense adulation and reverence. Carlton then recollects the events by informing me he had even put off a first date with his girlfriend as this was Town's first match of the season, he did not want to sleep in or have to get up early and miss the match.

The youth that day of the HYS met in the train station and numbered around fifty, they had also arranged to meet up with some of the older end in Peterborough. They descended upon Peterborough railway station and were surprised to find that no police waiting for them. They moved swiftly into the town centre and called at a pub. Everyone noticed that an eerie and solemn mood seemed to be hanging over the place. The lads could not believe what was going on, again with ease and no police about they roamed about at their will. They then made their way to the known Peterborough pub and found that that it had no police presence and the doors were locked. A few of their boys looked puzzled at the HYS behaviour in the pub windows; the HYS could not believe what was happening. They just roamed around and some of the lads with this being a sunny day decided not to bother with the match. They decided to stay on a boat, which was a bar by the river and were then approached by Huddersfield's main football copper and Peterborough's copper. The boys were informed that only twelve coppers had been assigned to match duty because the rest had been previously looking for the two girls' bodies and the force being strained. The full story then being told left the lads feeling a little low and phone calls to the rest of the lads at the match and other pubs were made. The Police were then informed that the lads agreed to leave straight away and not cause any bother to which both Police enforcements gave them respect and credit for. A couple of the lads arrested down at Peterborough later informed the lads that a group of police had a woman sat in a cell surrounded with the door open. It was later learned that this was that monster of a cow Maxine Carr.

As they managed to get away earlier than intended they called at the Elephant and Castle in Wakefield which is home to the Wakefield whites, just to see if they could make a day of it but no one was available. Back in Huddersfield the mood changed when the shout came up that Manchester City were in a bar just up the road. The lads fired up and the bouncers would not let them in, City were giving it at the windows, one of the youth saw that some roadwork's were being carried out and informed the rest of the firm. Anything the youth could get their hands on went through the same window that the City boys were behind. The red and white barriers were the only testament of where the road work equipment vanished to, they where sticking half out of this pubs window. City never ventured out and the youth did one when the sirens were heard.

As I have stated previously, tactics now play a major part in hooligan warfare and with the invention of the mobile this has been the biggest ally to plan, arrange and conjure up these clandestine meetings, although it has been some of these mobs' downfall as well. I have also overheard a story between the youth where Town was away at Macclesfield one year and only a few of the boys had made the journey away. They received a call from a neighbour of ours for a meet as this certain team had been playing at Preston. What the boys had not told them was that they only numbered a dozen and this lot had around eighty. They told this firm that they would meet them. One of the HYS then had a brilliant brainwave, they found out what time this other firm's train would be in another part of Yorkshire and decided to ambush them by surprise. A few calls were made to the Crescent and they arranged to meet the other lads at the new arranged venue. The lads who had been to the match pulled short their journey and made their way to the new venue by taxi to avoid any suspicion or the chance of being caught.

They met the rest of the lads in a pub outside this station and the local youth of this particular town noticed that Huddersfield were in town. Huddersfield was asked what was going down and the locals were informed. They laughed at this and a few of them agreed to join the ranks which now numbered twenty five plus.

They then proceeded to line the station tooled up to the nines and stood in the shadows. Around five minutes went and the sound of the train was to be heard. The other firm had been taunting the boys by mobile and were taking the piss, the train rolled in and the carriages with this firm pulled up, they did not stand a chance with the onslaught bestowed upon them. As quick as the HYS hit this mob they were just as thorough in their exit to avoid any police capture. This mob knew they had been done good style and it really knocked them off their perch and dented their reputation, they also needed plenty of bandages and ointment.

On away days the lads as other firms are usually accompanied by a couple of spotters from the local constabulary. From what I have heard these lads are on name terms and have got to know them well because they see them on a weekly basis. It's all a game of cat and mouse to out do the police from both firms and the lads will try anything and go to any lengths to get a meet. Plans are usually made well in advance and pubs outside of the city or town centres are chosen and both sides will go all out. The law is not daft and they keep the firms under surveillance, as they also know who everyone is. As I have said the mobile phone is the lads' biggest weapon and it has been known for other firms to arrange meets for the two consulting firms on that day in case anyone is listening in on them. Another great feat for the lads was Oldham away. The law had expected the firm to travel by bus and coaches to Oldham. This place being a hot spot enough in the year two thousand and two to two thousand and three season, the old bill does not want any more bother to ignite it all up again. It's the first match of the season and the HYS are really buzzing, it's one of the lads' last outing and it's his birthday. He has bought his lad a season ticket and the rest of the lads want to make it a good one for him. Initially the plan for the day was to organise a few transit vans but this fell through, the law was privy to this information and was spotted as usual parked just up the road from the Crescent ready to follow the lads. This was a category A match and they did not want to be caught cold over this one. The lads went to a totally different pub for the meet. They organised every taxi they could muster from around Huddersfield and went to the outskirts via a different route to a place called Chadderton. They went into this pub next door to a building site one of the lads had been working on. The football was on, the landlord was ok and the lads waited for their numbers to grow. One of the locals was noticed to have a Paul Shark jumper and the lads struck up conversation with him. He informed them that he was Man City and that he hated Oldham.

When all the firm turned up the mobile was busy with the Oldham firm. The venue was sorted and the time agreed. The Man City lad and his brother then proceeded to take the HYS to the arranged meet. All the bottles and pool balls etc had also strangely decided to follow the lads for some unknown reason. The mood was now changed and it was down to business, great the lads thought, no law, the beer flowing and the chance of a good kick off on the first day of the season. They headed off through an estate and were spotted by a routine local police car. The lad and his brother pointed to a playing field where the pub was next to. Knowing that they had been spotted they knew it would only be a matter of time before the football plod would be there. The tempo was lifted as they approached the pub, Oldham were out to meet the HYS in what looked like even numbers, bobbing all about. The roar was up and the HYS streamed into them, the local law was turning up in force and all hell was on. Oldham on home ground was trying to put up a good show but the HYS did not move an inch backwards and were hungrier for it. One of the HYS had his leg half-bitten off by a police dog, the HYS had now got the upper hand but the law was taking control. The lads tried doing one but were penned in into the car park until the football plod came. They were informed that it was first thought that they were BNP as the estate they had marched through was mainly Asian. This happened the previous year where the law did march them through another Asian area trying to ignite bother so that they could let fly. Oldham has always been a good row and at least they did the honours on turning out and standing. It just shows with a bit of good planning and luck, it turns out all right in the end.

Thinking about all of this made me think back to our day and I tried to recall when we had used a bit of the tactical manoeuvres. One or two instances were brought back to memory but I think it was Bradford City down at our place. We were on our way down and decided to walk towards Bradford road through the Beast Market. We knew or thought we might bump into some with them coming down this way. We also knew that City would be in the Market Tavern and also the Spinners Arms, which they always took over when they came down in the old days. We came round the corner from the wood merchants and Big K had spotted a group of Bradford's boys. Quick he says, hide in the electrical place gateway on the bridge, some hang back here, the others get over the other side of the road before they come. It was the perfect tactical pincer movement ever, we got them from three sides and they didn't know what hit them. Bradford put up a good show once they got their bearings but we had to be careful, as in all cases in these scenarios the directional movement of the ruck travelled up and down and sideways, but in this instance we drove them forwards over the bridge into sight of both the pubs with hundreds of their boys about and also the law. A big lad of theirs was having a right go back and I think Capper or big K gave him a good twat to which this lad came firing back again. The law had seen and heard the noise and a few more of their lads had also noticed. We dispersed into the crowds walking down and kept an eye on each other, a good little result and a first on a tactical move.

2000

Chapter Twenty-four
Old Hands and New Boys
The HYS

It's interesting when the younger crew start talking of and about the kick offs they have had with certain firms that you yourself have come across in the past. I just wonder what the past old boys of our time think about it and they must be the same as us and still turn out for the big ones. It's in your blood and at times when you reminisce with the lads you still have that urge to want it to happen again. Against Port Vale it was good to see all the old lads and quite a few of us stayed round Vale on the beer instead of going to the match. Word had got out that they knew the old firm was coming down and they had eighty lads about looking for a meet. We never saw anyone and we visited quite a few pubs. The laugh was how long we would keep going on, to still keep on having reunions until we are sixty and fighting their old boys with zimmer frames, you can imagine that with some of the lads that I know.

It's interesting when a new club come up from the lower division that are either new to the league or one that you have never come across before. I remember Wigan coming up into the league and us lot going over for the first time. No one really knew what to expect from the new boys and at this time in the early eighties it was known as a rugby area. The ground was in the middle of a built up housing area and nice little streets were all around, just the sort for the perfect little battle if it came. We got into the ground and found ourselves in their end. We were not to be disappointed and it soon kicked off with the Wigan lads who were well up for it. I remember a big gap between the two warring factions opening up and then both sets just went for it, well game for it they were. So it came as no surprise when Carlton told me of the trip down to Boston who themselves had just come up into the league. He agreed with me that some of the best outings can come from away days where you are really not expecting something rather than be let down on an arranged big event where you expect it to happen and nothing does or just a few skirmishes in a pub.

I think it was the first away day of the 2003 season and it was Boston. None of the lads through their contacts had heard anything about them and we were really resigned to looking at a piss up day with the hope of a meet with some other crew later. We decided to travel by mini bus and cars and landed in Boston at opening time. We had arranged to settle in a couple of pubs and keep contact with each other and not cause too much of a nuisance with a large gathering so that the police legged us off to the ground. We found a great pub and made ourselves very comfy in the beer garden enjoying the sun. The firm's numbers were growing and the phones were red hot. We were then joined by a few of the lads who had been scouting the area and were informed that Boston had a crew out and which pub they was in.

We decided to drink up and take a look at this lot. We noticed that no law was about and thought it could be the fact that coming from non league they were not expecting the extent of lads from Huddersfield that there was.

We arrived at this pub and again we never saw any law on the way or outside or in the vicinity of this gaff. We marched into the pub and noticed that the Boston lads were the likes of Chav's rather than a football firm, they numbered around fifteen plus and also had a pitbull with them. The Chav's kicked off and Huddersfield piled into them, the lad who had the pitbull let it off the lead and shouted "Get them" and the dog just sat down whimpering.

The Boston lads had no option but to do one and left the pub. Huddersfield's numbers were still increasing and they again resigned themselves to a day on the beer. Most of the lads decided to go onto the match and left a few of the boys still out on the beer.

The ground was a right old throw back to the eighties where you could walk all round. We had a good laugh and just as we were leaving the ground we got a phone call informing us that the Boston lads had caught the half a dozen HYS lads who had stayed out on the piss. They had come back ten minutes before the game had finished and kicked off with the few lads that we had left there. We marched on to the pub stirred up and just marched past the old bill and into this gaff. These lads were waiting for it and all hell then broke loose with everything flying all over, tables, chairs and bottles, when this stopped it was straight into them with boots and fists. They tried to put up a show but got it, we left via the back door as the old bill came storming in leaving the Chav's very bruised and battered.

We settled in another pub waiting for the league cup draw and picked Sunderland, I was informed that the old bill were after me for the little episode with the Chav's and swapped my shirt, but being the only dark skinned lad there and at six foot two I don't think my new identity would have fooled anyone.

We left Boston and just gave them a reminder of what to expect in the big boy's league and called off at Goole for a few bevvies. Nothing came off and the highlight was spiking one of the lads' drink with viagra and getting him going, he had a most uncomfortable ride home.

There are certain teams around that you know you will have a good chance of a row if the situation has been arranged well. This had been the case and was one of the big ones that was bound to kick off, Hull City was coming to Town. Now I myself remember this lot from our days and they were always up for it and had a good firm. It's a rough hole and always has been. We once went by train and had a good crew of around fifty of us. We had been spotted by a young couple of lads and knew the word would be out. We ended up splitting up into two groups and our little lot went one way and "Basher" and the rest of the crew went another way.

We had a good day's drinking and I remember waking up in a pub, the lads had left me there for the laugh asleep. I went walking up the road and found the lads who had just seen off a group of Hull lads who had been beating a couple of Town youngsters, Ginger Dave and his mate. As we were walking up to the ground, the other group in taxis went past, they stopped and got out. They had just taking a bit of a pasting in a pub. The lads had been sussed out and knew the game was up when a lad came into the pub and looked around. He went over to a table and told a couple of lovebirds to drink up and get out. As soon as they had gone the Hull stormed the pub and the lads had all on. They managed to hold it and the law arrived. We travelled on up the road to be greeted by around one hundred plus Hull who were hell bent on giving it to us. We must have only been fifty yards away and it looked like this was going to be a good one, Basher was screaming the odds and geeing everyone up, the law appeared in big numbers to avert what could have been a big one. Basher and his girlfriend both got arrested as he tried to get at them. So it was no great surprise when Carlton brought up Hull. Everyone was hyped up and the lads knew they had a very good chance of a meet with the phone calls being made. Around thirty plus of the youth had turned up at Wetherspoons and the numbers were made up to around forty plus with some of the older end. Dead on eleven Hull phoned to say they were here and the lads bounced out into the main road to be confronted by around five Hull, these soon became twenty odd and they were game enough wanting HYS to come at them. The lads went forward and were then greeted by a massive roar, the rest of the Hull mob came round the corner and in total they numbered around one hundred and twenty. The HYS went streaming in and a nice little battle was just beginning when the old bill turned up in full force, stopping any real outbreak of a mass kick off. This in today's modern day football violence is all part and parcel of the game and is expected. One of the lads who was with the Town that day also follows Stoke and was on the phone with his mates telling them in disbelief that they had been at it at eleven that morning in the town centre. Most of the lads went to the match and a few of the other lads stayed out drinking, trying to organise another kick off with the Hull. Came the second half, the lads started leaving the ground in very small groups and all met up in a pub up Leeds road. Word had gone round and the firm's ranks were swelling every five minutes and by the end of the match the HYS were numbering around one hundred and fifty plus. Hull where in contact with the lads and informed them which way the old bill were escorting them back.

The Huddersfield laid in wait making themselves as inconspicuous as possible, hiding in every little nook and cranny. They knew which side road the Hull were being brought up and could see the Hull firm being escorted by around five horses and other police on foot. The roar went up and the HYS made their move with bottles, glasses chairs and anything else that could be launched at them. Such was the ferocity of the attack and barrage that not only did Hull do one down the road but the old bill was following them as well. The reinforced police re-grouped and charged back into the Huddersfield with baton charges firstly from the horses and then the footmen. The Huddersfield dispersed and called it a good day with a few beers which ran into the night, Hull knew who came out on top that day and again when we went over there for the return match which was Hull's promotion season. Again it kicked off good style and the youth really made a name for themselves as Mr C quoted in his chapter. The older ones watching as the youth stream rolled the Hull crew in the car park. The older ones sensing something was wrong stood back and realised it was a set up with the law. This did not stop the Youth from their objective and purpose and a raging and bloody running battle took place for over five minutes with no police intervention.

Chapter Twenty-five

England and Respect
The HYS

Although times have changed and there isn't the same
level of violence between groups at the England matches
you still get and always will, a certain amount between
the firms. The Huddersfield Youth Squad has had their
share and still has respect within the set up. The difference
we have also seen is with Wembley stadium not here and
the games being played at different venues and the north
for once getting their fair share of the spoils with games
up here.

The youth squad has been going to the England
matches since two thousand and one of the first games
the lads went to was at Liverpool when England played
the Czech Republic. They had a large number and most of
them had no tickets. The day was set out in the bars and
in Witherspoons we enjoyed a beer with the Everton lot
who some of the lads knew. We got on the train and were
heading home when a slagging match started with Villa

(these second class brummies again!) and it was all set to kick off when the old bill came into calm the situation. We stopped at Warrington and noticed a large group of really ugly and nasty looking lot get on. On hearing our Yorkshire accents, these lot at first thought that we were Leeds and because this lot were Manchester United's top lads, they proceeded to fire into the HYS and also started flashing blades and verbal abuse stating that us lot were all a set of pakkies. Once they found out that we were Huddersfield things calmed down and upon approaching Oxford street station where both firms had to change trains we were warned to stay on the train for our own safety while they rampaged it. As the last lot were getting off someone from the HYS threw a bottle at them and more followed. The crazy Mancs started attacking the train with bottles, luggage trolleys and fists and gave the carriage a right pasting with the lads trying to hold them off. Luckily for the HYS the driver had then locked the doors and after a few minutes took off. When the lads got home phone calls were made to this mob by lads who had allegiances with both firms and the HYS were informed that the Mancs had given them respect for there brave stand of thirty seconds (and five minutes tactically backed on the train)

Another big turn out was at the last game before qualification for Japan in Manchester. We were playing Greece and needed a point to qualify. We ended up around the Deansgate and Piccadilly area and headed into Manchester. I will never forget the free kick that Beckham scored to get us qualified and the pub erupted with broken glass all over and ceiling tiles all over the place.

After the match we headed back up to Deansgate and ended up in a pub called the Thirsty Scholar. It was full of lads who we soon found out to be Man City. They soon found out that we were Huddersfield and tension was rife with the City boys calling us Munich's because it was known of affiliations between the two clubs.

Things settled a bit when the story was told of the events that took place after the England game with the Man U boys at Oxford Street station and that after all we were Huddersfield Youth. You could tell that quite a few of them still wanted it to kick off with us and the tension was still there. Just at this point a lad flew in the pub and shouted that the Munich's were here, we all looked at each other and knew it was pay back time.

On a friendly with Holland as you would expect all the lads were in Amsterdam sampling the goods on offer, word came round that the Turks had knifed a Geordie lad. We kept meeting a few lads in every bar we visited and as the beer was flowing people were getting angrier. There has been a lot of friction between the Turks and us. We all hold respect for the way the Arsenal lads sorted them out after what happened to the two Leeds lads. Anyway we visit this other bar and a few Reading boys were game to join us and find this gang of Turks. We visited a few bars and spent a couple of hours looking for them to which they had become invisible. We ended up in another bar and Oxford were in, well these boys and the Reading lads had business to sort with each other so we left them to it, no need to get involved with other people's business. We then ended up on our own again and were really smashed. It ended up with just two of us trying to find our Hotel which we found out that there were another twenty or so that had the same name. We ended up brawling with a carload of locals that had tried to run us down, the law was there in an instant and me mate got nicked. I couldn't remember anything in the morning and when the rest of the lads turned up asking for me mate I couldn't tell them.

I asked Carlton which crew he held respect for and also which crew gave Huddersfield respect on an event. One lot he has respect for was Wrexham. It was the end of the season and they had arranged to meet in Chester. Wrexham had a young crew and Huddersfield thought it was all mouth and bravado from this lot. I will give them their due, they did turn up at the arranged place and they did come and stand. We were outnumbered but had some of the older end with us and the experience again paid off which is noted in chapter twenty five.

I know of all the stories over the years and up to this present date on battles between Leeds and Huddersfield and it was this team that actually rang the next day and gave us respect for the way in which we conducted ourselves. Town had been playing some nondescript and we knew Leeds would be passing through later. It was arranged with Leeds agreeing to turn up for a rumble. Town had a good crew and all the lads were buzzing at the prospect of a meet, time passed and it looked as though Leeds were not going to turn up. The numbers of the youth squad started to dwindle and they moved onto another pub. Leeds had rung to say that they were still coming but it could have just been a ploy to wind the lads up.

The Youth by now numbered around thirty five and word came that they were in town. The lads popped onto the Crescent were they were informed that Leeds had a very good crew and that Town should leave this one alone.

The lads started walking to the next pub and came across the Leeds who where down the bottom end of town and numbered around eighty, one of their top lads was swinging a buffet above his head with one hand, the Youth knew that this lot meant business and thought fuck it, let's give it them. Huddersfield ran down towards the Leeds and for the first thirty seconds or so had the better of this mob, Leeds knew they outnumbered us and came storming back at us. The battle lasted around five minutes before the old bill turned up in numbers and restored peace. They had the better of us in the end because of their numbers but rang the next day to say what a good performance we put up and that Leeds had a lot of respect for the show we put on with the numbers we had.

2000

Chapter Twenty-six
Dads and Lads
The End is Nigh

What makes a person regardless of their background colour or creed associate into what others deem as mindless violence and become addicted to football hooliganism? I have not the answer and neither have the sharp-witted so called experts. I watched a programme a couple of weeks ago about the six fifty seven Portsmouth crew and its brief was about one of the original boy's son following in his father's footsteps and the son was now part of the new generation of the six fifty seven crew.

The same I would think must apply to other firms where this hereditary behaviour takes place as we ourselves have the same scenario with several Dads and Lads.

I remember talking with Mr C several years ago about this and we both agreed the first instance that you want your off-spring to be better, but as they get older and the stories they hear between the lads of old etc must have some bearing on it as well. They will go their own way.

I myself had an experience with David. It was Wolves at home and as usual they had brought a big crew up. Through the game the usual gestures and songs were aimed at each set of fans. I recall telling David that if it kicks off after the match to go down to the Bradley Mills club at the end of the road where we all met up for a drink afterwards.

It kicked off big time outside and I recall standing there with one of the lads watching. I turned around and David was gone. Thinking he had gone onto the club with some of the other lads, we went back to the club to find that he was not there. Giving it ten minutes and still no show, I went onto the Ropewalk pub next to the ground where we had gone before the match, he was not there. I repeated this feat twice and by this time I was a little worried and more so at what his mother would do to me than anything else.

I was in the car and pulling out of the car park when a group of around twelve young ones came past with David.

He got into the car and said, fucking brilliant that, I have just been involved in two skirmishes with the HYC boys and the young Wolves lot. I was gob-smacked and besides telling him off for swearing, I made him promise not to tell his mother. As it was he took another route and did not enter the world of hooliganism.

Ellis as I have written has the same with Jodie. Mark's outlook on it all is the same, he recalls Port Vale last year. I went with Jodie and around ten of his pals. It reminded me of the old days on the train with him and his mates having a laugh. They did not mind me coming along, as they know I am nuts anyway. All goes well and after the match we head back into town and after the first boozer we noticed we have been spotted. We kick it off and these young lads don't mess around, stools through the window and the lot. We got told that this particular bunch are Stoke looking for a bit, well they got it whoever they were. Regardless of my past with town, Jodie will do what he wants anyway. You can only point and guide them in the right direction and see which path they take.

Some people look too much into it and if two lots of lads want to fight what's the problem.

I honestly believe that the end is near and that football hooliganism is dying out. Mr C who started out in this game just after I did has been active from that time in the late seventies up to this present time also shares the same sentiments with me to a degree.

I remember Mr C at the beginning of the eighties; he was part of a mob from Brighouse and had allegiances with Syko and Locky. Both Mr C and his brother D were well-known and very game lads indeed. One of my favourite recollections is when we went to Manchester on the train. We were playing City at the time when we lost ten-one. We had a crew of around twenty five of us and we were making our way through the centre between pubs. As we were walking up the main street, a couple of wide boys were giving it the come on, Mr C youngest brother and I decided to have it out with these two. We followed them up the road and after a few swapped punches and back pedaling with these two we distanced ourselves without really knowing from the rest of the crew. One of these lads suddenly flew into a pub and within seconds we were confronted by around twenty Mancunians baying for blood. They came at us and R flew into them. This was his first outing away and whether he thought that this was what you did, full marks, but being so outnumbered and seeing the danger, on occasions like this the best part of valour is to leg it. I managed to grab him and we ran. As we were legging it down the road, I could see the boys wandering up. I shouted the alarm and Mr C had been keeping an eye on things all the time, was one of the first to the scene.

R went down and I stopped and turned and went back at them, by this time the boys were with us and a full-scale battle on the high street took place. Shoppers were scattering everywhere and people were screaming, traffic stopping and so on. Daisy one of the Brighouse lads had been stabbed in the head with an umbrella and the best sight was seeing Nick and Fountain knocking two of these Mancunians cold out simultaneously. The law turns up and after a few minutes order was restored.

I got a good bollocking from Mr C for falling into that old trap as he called it.

We went off down the road and had a beer in the nearest pub. Two of their boys came in on a scouting mission and we expected the same upon leaving the pub, nothing. We ended up staying out on the piss and missed the match, which we were glad to that point.

I asked Mr C on the three generations of crews that he has seen come through and which in his mind has been the better and what he considers the best era. Mr C stated that "each and every crew has had its different strengths and weaknesses. The eighties were my preference he says. We had a good solid crew and we all enjoyed the away days better. No mobiles and the thought of what was to come. It was mainly to get out on the piss and have some fun. Whatever came we dealt with, as you know we have had some spine chilling moments.

We used to do all sorts of silly and stupid things and one of the funniest things was, all though some people will not agree, is when we used to appoint a leader of the crew for the day.

We had to follow his instructions to the tee regardless and the day was left to him to organise. When our D was made leader for Sheffield United away there were around twenty five of us and we went by train. A great day out and after the match we started making our way back. We broke away from the crowd and headed back towards town. We then realised that behind us was a rather large mob of their boys, then one of the lads shouted we've got company up front. There was also banking to the right and yes you've guessed it, more of the fuckers. Fountain then pops up and said, that's the last time you're being leader for the day, you've led us into a right trap here D, what's our course of action now then. D looks around and assesses the situation; we go through the front lot at speed he barks out. The adrenaline is flowing at an alarming rate, thoughts of hospital food and this is a bad one and will we make it are going through individual minds. The shout goes up and it's the charge of the light brigade, into the valley of death. Sheffield are waiting, massed across the road bobbing and taunting, we are getting closer, as a unit the crew charge through at speed and manage to break through without any major injury. Mr C acknowledges the Sheffield boys on that day, full marks to them, they could have annihilated us, it was something of a humiliation though, some of them had taken their shoes off and were clouting us with them, they could have gone to town on us." He agreed that times have changed and again stated "the late eighties and early nineties were different. The fights were being arranged on a more regular basis and a military style organisation was being seen.

We were no different and with the birth of the HYC it was good to see these lads in action.

This lot was different and malevolent to the degree of setting pubs on fire and intent to cause damage who ever got in their way. These lads really wanted to let the other teams just know who was boss and did so on a regular basis. I have also heard some very good accounts of them from the England set up and how they made a name for themselves.

Then we saw the re-birth in the middle to late nineties of us lot and the young ones called us the OAPs and then into the over forties club. Again laughs were had by all and this is what I would consider the best rumble that I have ever been involved in was at Wolves. You hear and read stories of fifteen lads standing against two hundred and think bullshit and fuck that but it did happen and what a fucking victory that turned out to be. We really held our own that day and I still can't understand why we did not get smashed to bits especially outside the pub.

As we came into the millennium and up to this present time, more and more people were getting nicked. Numbers started to decrease but town still had a decent mob.

Hull away the other year just goes to show how the police have after all these years started the crack down. After the match the Hull lads were in the big car park, now us older lot knew something was amiss, they let all the Huddersfield youth into this car park and a raging battle that lasted just under ten minutes, with no police intervention. The battle was filmed and dawn raids months after took place, which really was the demise of the Huddersfield youth, a lot of them received banning orders.

The last big one was Wrexham away last year, it was the last match of the season, and it was organised to meet with them in Chester after the match.

Apparently the numbers we had were mixed heavily to the older side, some thirty and around twenty young ones. They turned up at the venue, which was at the Witherspoons

They brought around ninety to one hundred plus but were all young ones. They got a good hiding but fair game for showing and having a go. Experience pays off and it showed that day as well. Again it's only the other week that the law so I am informed has started pulling for that one.

The banning orders with filming and CCTV have all but killed it off now and yes, I agree it's on the way out.

From what I hear some of these lads now ring up other crews for the off just to let a bit of steam off, but that's not the same is it, it's a shame but that's life"…

I myself along with other people from this book have no regrets and although the majority of us grow through and away from the front line and move on. Who out there who have been associated with this can ever turn around and condone it, how many times when we all meet up do we laugh when reminiscing about it all and when we see or hear something still connected with this say, go on lads or feel proud.

The great Bill Shankley once wrote Football is a game of life and death.

Hooliganism has been a lot of people's life, is this then sadly the death?

Chapter Twenty-seven
One From The Boys
Mick Basher Bennett

In all firms you have the Mr Big. The one lad that always leads from the front and will inspire other lads in times doubt. Through the eighties I think most people will agree with my sentiments on this.

This is meant as no disrespect to other lads who could have matched Mick at times and who were just as brave.

Mick was a big lad, over six-foot with a medium build, and hands the size of shovels. He along with Oscar were the first ever two people to be arrested on video evidence. The match was down at home against Leeds United. Mick was a quite lad at heart and would do anything for anyone. He would always help the underdog and not flinch in the face of adversity. Unbeknown to many Mick was very articulate in many respects outside of football life. I went over to South East Asia with Mick and we had a ball of a time with Knighty, Paul Trav, Darky and Chris Soap . On the way back we were asked to move from the seats we were sat in by a worried air stewardess as the "London lot" always sat in these. Mick replied very nicely to the young girl, that the "Huddersfield lot" now occupied them and would the rest of the flight and not to worry too much about a set of silly cockneys and that he would look after the situation. When he stood up, I think she got the drift. Funny, the London lot never mentioned anything either when they boarded.

Mick was known as Basher to many in our fraternity. His main core of friends from the earlier days were Patty, Milo, Dave, Joe, Tats, then Andy (bruiser).

They were a well-known lot and through the years I have befriended all of them and they are a good set of lads.

I have been and seen countless episodes with Mick but one that always brings me to a shiver is when we were walking up from the station in Chesterfield one year. A big group were coming down a side street and when they saw us lot they started running towards us, Mick seeing this lot, grabs hold of me with one hand and charges up the road, my feet did not touch the ground for twenty yards or so before he then put me down, the only reason he did was because the group that were charging down were the Brighouse lads, I hate to think what would of happened if it had been the other lot, he would have probably used me as a baton. He was a great lad and is sadly missed by all.

The Silver Fox's Story

They called him Tiger in his younger days, cunning, stealth like and fast. He was fearless and could smell or spot a potential fight a mile off. I remember this chap with a flick head hairstyle, we did not have many in Huddersfield and he would gel in with other groups unnoticed and then strike like a panther.

When the red mist sets in with this fella no prisoners are taken and it's fuck the consequences like the time against Rotherham and again on the pitch at Huddersfield against Millwall, firing in against loads of them, he ended up getting nicked that match for belting the assistant coach! I could go on and on, the best accolade to bestowed upon him whilst speaking with Peanut about the book and him was "he was our best hooligan in his time"

The Fox would pounce where others did not, he was tricky and whilst a mob would bait another with the law around, he would beckon one of their boys away for a one to one or maybe a three on three type of brawl, he had a knack of this,

We laugh at the Grimsby ruck, while it was all going off, he still had time to dip his fingers in the till behind the bar or so the rumour has it.

It was the early seventies when the Fox started frequenting the Leeds road ground. He recalls the Middlesborough crew coming down all dressed in white type boiler suits and the Forest boys all wearing crombies. He says, "I first remembers the Golcar lads with the problems and fighting with the Almondbury lot. We all started going off together and have had some good fun. There has been some scary moments and very laughable ones as well. Some of them stick in your head and one in particular I can recall was at Chesterfield in the Crooked Spire. It was the usual scenario of beer and cards and we ended up in there after the match. We had a dozen or so in numbers and had noticed a few of their boys. Their numbers were swelling and we thought fuck it we had better get this lot fucked before they start with us. They were headed by a big bald headed chap who for some reason just jumped up and shouted "attention" to the rest of his crew, now whether that was his command for them to start or what I do not know, but we gave it them good style. Nothing left of the pub, the jukebox so I gather was left lying on top of the bald headed geezer's head, wasn't shouting much after that. Good days and still are".

Bullit

My first recollection of this chap was in the late seventies. Bullit is not the tallest of chaps but a very squat Aryan looking type, hard and fast, hence the name bullet. In all the time I have known him he has never flinched in the face of adversity. He is a big team player and would not leave anyone in the dire.

He has a dry sense of humour and is very witty with the one-liners and a strong believer in the brother-ship of friends. He always had time to speak with you and I always remember him against the Villa mob at Blackpool. At one point I can remember backing off a little as the two groups squared up for the dozenth time and Bullit who came up behind me just said, "we don't step back Tel boy, it's forward all the way, get fucking stuck in". That type of sentiment is as good as a good kick up the arse and was what Bullit was all about.

Bullit and Peanut started coming down in the mid seventies and teamed up with Syko and Fozzer a while later, then we all amalgamated into our own team. Bob laughs at recalling first noticing us lot, "you were always at it with the Almondbury lads". When I told Bob of the book, I knew what the response would be. He was one hundred percent behind me, unlike a few who had mixed reactions to this. "Get it told Tel Boy and fuck 'em". He along with the Fox were the first two I interviewed and this certainly helped the nerves with the others that were to come. Bob recalls his best of the best with a jubilant smile, "two of London's top firms were fought in the same day and as he put it, the gods were on our side that day.

It was Charlton away and we all went down on the train, supping all round London and the Cockney Pride. We did not encounter anything till we got to the ground. What made us laugh that day was that a big mob of West Ham was down there, we were slugging it out all through the match; I got lifted although not arrested. Outside all the way to the tube, we were at it with the West Ham lad's, we had a mob of around thirty five to forty odd of us, tidy, we held our own that day and were really knacked by the time we got on the tube.

We were all just lazing and telling the usual jokes and having a laugh, some of the lads were nearly asleep, heads on the window, when we approached this station, around forty lads poured onto the tube and shouted, come on, we're Millwall, we were alive in seconds and straight into them, we gave them no mercy, it was toe to toe and real slugging, they put up a decent show but after a few stations they legged it, apart from one of them who was left on the carriage", he chuckles at remembering this and says, "well at least they knew who they had come up against eh, the lad shit himself, that was enough for us, he wasn't belted, what was the point, he'd seen it dished to his mates", I agreed with his next sentence and most from my era would also say the same "what I liked about those days was that nothing was organised, no mobiles in them days, the fun and the buzz was an away day, like we used to on the Friday night trains, into Soho and then on the beer after a breakfast, the thrill was who we would meet, that was the best part of it".

Mr. A

Mr. A is the one person who I have known throughout my whole life. We lived a few doors away from each other in our childhood. We are the same age and from those early days we have remained very good friends. I remember the fire engines turning up by the dozen one day after the embankment at the back of our houses being on fire. I ran to Mr. A house to get him out, to see this exciting event taking place. He was not allowed out, as it was he who was the fire-starter! We laugh about this now. He moved away and the next recollection I had of him was on a Hanson bus to an away match.

We soon realised who each was and over the years picked up the friendship once again. He seemed to have a knack of pulling me out of the shit in scrapes and we both laugh at the time we went down to Aston Villa. We could not remember where we had parked the van and spent what seemed at eternity walking round the terraced streets around the ground. We numbered three with Peanut's brother Paul and a pal just behind us, every street corner was the same with big gangs of Villa boys eyeing us up. We could tell we were being watched and mobile phones were ringing everywhere and eyes upon us. In my mind I kept thinking, this is it, this is our time, comeback a hundred times over. I kept bugging Mr. A, where the fuck is that van, look 'Tel boy he says knowing quite well we could be picked off at any time, if they come, knock on the first door we see and I will hold them off. As it happened they did not take their opportunity and fuck us, we saw the van and a long sigh of relief came from all of us, but that's the kind of lad he is, he put us first. It was great and we had loads of laughs he recalls and the team we had has to be the best of all times. We have come up against them all and held our own. The one time I actually thought I was going to get it big time he says was against Tranmere away. We came up against them in that big park on the way down from the ground to the railway station. It kicked off and it was good hand-to-hand combat, I remember the Silver Fox in with their lot with his flick head haircut, just looked like one of them and then pouncing. We ended up running them onto the streets. I remember being out of breath and realising that I was way in front of anyone else, the Tranmere lot knew this and came back for the kill.

I thought that this was it, I couldn't run and lent against the wall with my back, all of a sudden and out of nowhere came big K with a Charlie and smashed it into the head of the first one that was upon me. No regrets and I would not change anything.

Max

Max is one of the original Golcar boys and one of the top men from our crew. He was one of the youngest of our lot in the earlier days and would be the first to fire in. Shouts of Max, Max would often be heard when one of us was in trouble and he always obliged. He is one of my closest friends with our wives being best buddies and has helped me through some difficult times, the latest as stated in the last chapter.

Through the early years he was like the rest of us with the matches but soon drifted past this before most of us. He would turn out for the big ones and all the stag parties and so on. One recollection was when we had Pompey up here the second time, this big twat and his mates was coming for me and Max had just got into the terracing and was charging down, Max I shouted, twat that big cunt, with this he turned and the group that was heading for me looked on in amazement as he fired into them all. I will also never forget his face being belted into the cell bars in Bridewell as I looked up from the cell floor from my beating. Time and time again until the marks were left on his face those bastards banged him. His best in my eyes was when we were at York, I can't remember how but he had to have a sling on his arm through the match. Everyone was on the pitch at the end of the match and York came to join us, Max was running round twatting all and sundry, as soon as a copper was about he would put his arm back in the sling and claim innocence, he got away with this till order was restored.

Ricky

Another of the Golcar originals and was affectionately known in the earlier days as one of the Wong brothers after the gang of Chinese in the film the Wanders. I had the pleasure of working and playing football with this little hard twat. He would always go in hard regardless of what and take the consequences as they came. A real good friend between the families and as I have said, we would often take our mothers on the piss with us in the earlier days. Ricky's fighting exploits are legendary and he was always to be found in the thick of it. We played Bradford on a night match and the in thing at the time was donkey jackets, a mass brawl erupted and then the gap appeared, me and Ricky ended up with all the Bradford lads with all our mates over the other side, we managed to get out of that one ok. He has had more black eyes than anyone else I know and owes me at least twenty jumpers from the early days. My personal favourite with Rick has got to be the time we went up to Carlisle. Around twenty of us ended up a bit of a distance from the ground in this boozer. We were keeping our eye on the situation as this pub was getting full with all kinds of lads. Several of these were National Front boys and they started talking with Rick, wrong man to strike a conversation up with on that subject, he fucking hated this lot with a vengeance. He just butted the first one nearest to him and that kicked it off for starters. As usual with this type of thing, it ended up with half the pub outside and a nice little brawl got going. The law turned up and we started making our way to the ground. We then came across some of the Carlisle crew and it kicked off again, I cant remember who, but I recall a crate full of empty milk bottles turning up and being used in that little encounter. We held our own very well on that event.

Ellis

The fucking Daddy, a lot of respect goes for this fella from all the Golcar boys and the earlier Town lads. One of the fore founders of our original Golcar troop and a man on a mission in the earlier days.

I had the pleasure of being best man for him and although through the years we lost touch, if we see him and Carol down the Town the old times flood back. To epitomise this lad would take an eternity and I will never forget the time against Bolton Wanderers when Ellis and Mick flew into the lot of them and for thirty seconds had the better of them. He is coming on the Port Vale reunion and like the rest of us is buzzing like mad. He still likes to be involved and has a never say die attitude. In his own words " I don't regret a fucking thing and I would not change anything from these days, I have a lot of friends and memories, fuck 'em".

Willy

Like brothers in the early days, again another outing as best man with this chap, to which I was honoured. One of my best mates and although we have gone on different paths through the years, we manage to keep in touch and have a good laugh about it all. Willy had a good right hook that could knock them out with one punch and like Ellis still has the occasional brawl. His statement was that our story should be told and that he enjoyed all of it and would not change anything at all (well maybe the Torquay bit). The friendship and laughs will never get beaten by anything and although today's lads are different, we still had the best crew.

Irish

Irish was a well-known lad within the Huddersfield crew. His pranks are legendary like the time in Torquay when he was off loaded in a dinghy and cried out that he could not swim as the dinghy drifted out to sea. He was one of the first lads I met in the mid seventies and was a good mate of Ellis. Like Ellis he was a smallish stocky type of lad with a hoarse voice and always was there in the thick of it. Through the late seventies and early eighties he always seemed to be around but then as most it was only every now and then that I saw him. The next time was in the late eighties when we played Sheffield United who had brought down a younger new crew who were well up for it as usual. All of a sudden he was there when it kicked off against this crew on Leeds road in the central reservation just past the Spinners Arms and again he was in the middle of it. Irish will be another of the old crew at Port Vale and talking of our time he recalls seeing me as a young curly haired lad who was always up for a laugh. He laughs at the time up at Darlington when I got flattened but like he says, "once we knew you were not with us we went straight back at them". I have to agree with Irish on his outlook in which he says, "the old days were better than today, they were marvellous and no drugs, the football was our drug and the old gang were the best, everyone looked after each other, it was in your blood. I remember going to watch Man U against Sheffield Wednesday when Town's match was postponed, it was garbage, over 48,000 fans there, it was not the same, I couldn't cheer, it was not Town. The week after it was Town back at home with 4000 there, I was in my element then he says". The Fox has wound him up a bit with the book and his last words to me were " fuck them all Tel, put us on the map, we fucking deserve it, at least you have had the bottle to write the book and no one can take that away from you"

H

H is well known even to this day. He was one of the old boys and another lad who has done extremely well for himself. When I first started going down to Leeds road H was a well-known face. He came from Almondbury and used to get all the lads singing. They used to have a friendly rivalry against the Heckmondwike lads and the shout of Almondbury was greeted with "Wankers" and then the shout of Heckmondwike would be greeted with "Harriers" It was all good humour and at the forefront of it all was H. He would sing the give us an H song and everyone went quiet when it was sounded off. My best recollection was at Doncaster one Friday evening, town were losing and H just turned round and said, fuck it let's get a suicide squad and fuck the bastards, are you Golcar lot in, I ended up getting my arse bitten by a police dog that night and it fucking hurt.

H still turns out and we have a good laugh, he went to Swansea last season and asked me to give them boys a good write up on his behalf.

He was with a few pals in the Witherspoons bar down there when around thirty Swansea youth came in. They struck up a conversation with H and his mates and invited them to their pub. H was a bit apprehensive but they went. They were introduced to the Swansea firm and had their beer bought all night and stories swapped with the older end of Swansea and well looked after. H stated again that he was no hard man but loved the camaraderie of it all. The old days were great and it's still great to see the old faces when I turn up.

AJM

I have a lot of memories with this chap. AJM is one of the old brigade and still turns out week in and week out, home and away. We have organised a few trips between us and the over forty reunions, which have been a great success. He has seen the different Town firms come and go and again like everyone else says he would not change a thing. Bristol was a bad one but that's what happened in those days. He was down at Bournemouth this year and he could not believe it. It was just like the old days he says, Bournemouth had a new youth crew and it went off good style with the Town youth. The pub was smashed to bits and at the front of it all was an old boy, RJ. Just like the old days he informs me nothing changes although stricter policing and CCTV along with the banning orders have cut it all down. However, new generations always seem to come through and new faces appear to fill in the gaps.

Fountain and Nick

This book would not be complete without a mention of these two. Both played a big part from the late seventies up to the nineties. They were a better double act than Morecambe and Wise, Laurel and Hardy and Pinky and Perky and were the gamest of lads, each earning accolades in abundance in there own rights.

Nick looked like the milky bar kid and once his glasses were off that was it. Fountain was a scruffy elfin-faced lad who had a flacsum headbutt and both together was an awesome sight in action. I remember when we went to Manchester City and as told in the previous story we came across this mob that had belted me and Mr C brother R. In the midst of it all in the main shopping street, both

Steve and Nick had systematically thrown punches at different opposition only for these two lads to both get knocked out together, the sight of one of them flopping to the floor and half a second later his mate flopping over him was a sight to behold and will never be forgotten.

To me I will always remember Steve Fountain and his silly Cossack dance; he was always at the front of it and always had something silly to say on the outcome of any event. I remember him with Basher's crew in the early days and towards the mid eighties when we all amalgamated, he then took up with Nick. Unfortunately I have had no contact with him as he has been abroad for a while and those who know of him know why. He once gave me the name of Terry O Lion tamer for a bit of a do we had at the Montego club very late one Sunday night with my handy work with a bar stool buffet. There are countless episodes that I could mention about this pony-tailed urchin and it's a pleasure to write of him and to have been part of the same team with him. Nick was in the same mould with Steve and one of the big guns. He has broken and lost more pairs of glasses than Mr Magoo when the action has started. He along with the Gouch were the first lads in the eighties who we first got to know and he always had some silly statement on whatever happened that would cause roars of laughter from everyone. When I told Nick of the book he just laughed and said "fuck you, you little twat, you're not making any money out of me Enid Blyton".

Knighty

This fucker was the joker of the pack, he always had his knob out and would try to chat the girls with his chat up line of, Knighty's me name, and Fucking's me game whilst swinging his knob around like a helicopter blade. He was another of the original Golcar lads and although not one of the big guns he was a game lad when he had to be.

He was Mr Know it all and had the mouth to match his ego although his downfall was that he always put his foot in it with himself.

His favourite saying to the lads was, you knock them down and we will keep them down, this came about after one punch Milko gained his name against Lincoln at our place. Everyone knew Knighty and he was a larger than life character. I will never forget the day at Grimsby when half his face was sliced open and he still wanted to go at them, but he showed his worth at Blackpool on the front line when we were outnumbered against the Villa boys. He says of it all, "that he would not change anything and that we were the best".

Carlton

I got to know of Carlton through Syko and once a little trust was gained he gave me a very good insight of today's hooligan fraternity. Carlton respects the old boys and what we did in our time. He has laughed and listened with great interest and agreed that we have all the same thoughts and desires on this subject. He acknowledges the changes that have taken place and the new concepts that now take place in today's footballing firms. One of the best he recalls is when Cardiff's Soul Crew came to town. Town's firm met up in the usual abode of residence and rumour was rife that Leeds were coming over because of what had happened down at Cardiff. Whilst in another pub later that day, voices were heard that were not of our

English language What transpired was that several lads from Holland's club 20 firm that were in Liverpool on a stag party had seen the fixture and wanted to see some action, they were then invited by the HYS to watch the days unfolding events that were later to take place. On the way down to the match after a little contest with Cardiff another couple of firms, Man City and another was spotted, they had also come over to watch the events.

After the match the youth met with Cardiff and although Cardiff were outnumbered they put up a decent show but got it good style from the youth. Carlton points out that respect went to them for that. On returning into the town, the youth saw another group coming down to them, it turned out to be more Huddersfield who had just had it and sorted out Leeds. That was a good one in front of the other firms, I told him we did not have anything like that in our day and the nearest was when Leeds came over when we played Chelsea.

Good times and I really miss them Carlton informs me, he his still serving a banning order from the Wrexham away game that kicked off in Chester.

Tel Boy
Dream on

At Forty Six, I still feel the buzz like many other's who are the same age, it never leaves you and I am Huddersfield through and through. I still live in Golcar and I am proud that over the years we have produced some fine young men who have taken this road like ourselves and who have followed Town. The lads of today are different as their attitude and views are, but good on them. I enjoy going for a beer with them and at least they share a laugh when the old stories come out when the beer is in. What I like most is that our generation still get respect from these lads and that's how it should be. One little tale that always brings a smile is the time me and Pabs had built scaffolding round the Wheel pub for some work we were carrying out. We went for a drink to the pub on the Sunday morning and the pipes and wood boards were all over the place. The younger end of Golcar, Waddy, Poggy, the two B twins, Ginger Nick and the rest of them had been fighting with another village crew at an eighteenth and used this lot as weapons. Trying to play hell with them for the damage and mess, I was greeted with "Tel boy, what do you expect, would you rather we got belted", at least it made me laugh.

I have many great memories and it's not all been about violence, we have experienced a lot of laughs along the way, we have had some fantastic days and other days where the boot has been on the other foot. One of the most laughable experiences I came across has to be when we went down to Walsall one year, I had been thrown out of the ground, it had been kicking off inside and me and John Faye had just been thrown out. Outside was the Gouch and another couple of lads, we started walking towards the coach and the Gouch decided to have a shit. At this point about a dozen of their lads up the other end of the ground had seen us and were heading in our direction for the obvious. Come on Gouch I said they're coming, fucking wait he said I won't be long, fuck it, come on they're nearly here and they must have been only thirty yards away and the Gouch had just finished.

I can't remember if he even wiped his arse or not, his jeans came up and at this point a couple of punches had just been made and the usual bobbing about and so on. Just then with an almighty roar the giant rose and wadded into three of them playing fuck because he had been stopped short of a good shit, they soon legged it and all we could do was laugh. It's situations as these that then bring out the other factors that happened on the day. I can still see Knighty's face when we shoved him in a dryer in the launderette in Brighton one year because he was moaning of being wet, these are one timer's and one offs and no one forgets them.

There is a hell of a lot that has not been written in this book for the obvious reasons and countless episodes of others. To put one record straight though from a book of another firm, which indicated that they came into Huddersfield and walked over us, and even stayed the night around the town without being touched. Well Manchester City, you have been down to our place on a few occasions that I can recall. Each time we have held our own in your presence that I have witnessed with you. You did not write in your book about being pulled out of your vans on Leeds road in the late eighties at the lights across from the Spinners Arms have you, especially when we were outnumbered as well. You were giving it the big one and got a good taste of what we are capable of and at no point did anyone from Huddersfield see any of the so called 80 lads that stayed around the town centre that night after the match. Must have been a different town then eh mate…? The same applies to another book which states we are no more than a town of beer monsters, well my only answer to that one is we must be a good set of beer monsters to get sent back home from Holyhead because we were to hot to handle. On another note I would just like to say that over the years the best five teams or firms that I personally rate were Chelsea, Newcastle, Sheffield United, Barnsley and Birmingham.

All that I have written is of true standing and actual events. However some of the material I have written is over 25 years ago and the details may be a little crossed with duplication of visiting the same ground on different occasions, either that or the coke fucked me up good style. Other material I have taken is on that person's word and of true account.

I would also like to think that I have given an insight across the board with not putting us on a pedestal unlike other firms who have written that they are untouchable; because no matter who you are you always come across a better firm on a better day.

Some of the smaller footballing firms have been a better match for us than the so-called bigger ones and Barnsley and Bradford are testimony to that fact.

These boys along with us are more than capable of matching the big firms. I have many favourite rumbles and each one holds something special from that day that will always be remembered by but the biggest battle that I have just beaten is cocaine addiction. We all have skeletons in the cupboard, at some point down the years some of us slip down that slippery slope. I would like to thank the friends who helped me through this darkest hour and my workplace for the faith and understanding they showed me the same. They all know who they are and I would not recommend other people delving into that shit, it takes over and wrecks your life, family and mind.

Writing this book has to be one of the best things that I have ever done and again I cannot thank all the people that have been involved and that have been my friends through the years.

It has been great revisiting old times and seeing friends from many a year ago and making new ones with the youth of Huddersfield today.

We have a reunion at the end of March with two full coach loads of the over forties to Port Vale and we are really looking forward to that, so all that is to say for now is

We're Huddersfield
And fucking proud of it
COME ON

**The HYS at the Elephant and Castle
looking for the Wakefield Whites**

Terence OHagan

Huddersfield Youth 2000

HYS in Japan with some of the older end, "Duggie

HYS away at Oldham

Over 40s, Max, The Chef and Our Kid

Top, Gavin
Bottom, Carlton, Golcar and Huddersfield youth.

Golcar over 40s and youth, Shane, the Author and Pido at the
front, Lee, Liam, Norm, Max, Zoot and Willy at the back

The Only Two Gays in The Village – But Good Lads!

The football warrior

He's stopped it all but gets a text, he'd
thought he had his final slay.
Warrior, warrior we're playing away,
come once more and make our day
He leaves his dwelling and family behind; he
only has thoughts for the fight in mind.
He meets the pack and family he loves, they
joke and laugh, they're one of a kind.
A plan is made as the beverage is downed,
a call is made and off they go.
Their journey is short with stories of old,
it's off they get to meet their foe.
The mood has changed and the air is tense,
they are all pumped up and have pretence
They meet their foe but the plan is foiled,
also there is a police defence
A game of cat and mouse is played, in
hope of a meet before the match.
A call is made to wind them up, come on
you bastards we're on your patch.
It's nearly time for us to go, one last
attempt is planned and made
It's kick off time and it's gone all the way,
I turn and see the bloodied blade
Warrior Warrior what was the point,
a tearful family ask this day
From my grave is what I'd say, I took
allegiance and come what may

Printed in the United Kingdom
by Lightning Source UK Ltd.
120908UK00001BA/7